(Front Cover) Picture courtesy of Rusty Green
(Back Cover) European Hypomelanistic Courtesy of Shannon Brown; Vanishing Pattern Amelanistic Courtesy of Rusty Green; Tricolor Hypomelanistic Courtesy of Rusty Green; Peach Phase Tricolor Courtesy of Shannon Brown
(Opposite Page Top) Courtesy of Don Shores
(Opposite Page Bottom) Courtesy of Thomas Steffen

The Guide to

Honduran Milksnakes

A Collective History of Honduran Milksnakes for the Hobbyist

Douglas Mong
&
James Tintle

The Guide to Honduran Milksnakes
A Collective History of Honduran Milksnakes for the Hobbyist
Douglas Mong & James Tintle
ColdBlooded Publishing, LLC

All rights reserved. No part of this book may be reproduced or transmitted in any form or by any means, electronic or mechanical, including photocopying, recording or by any information storage and retrieval system, without written permission from the author, except for the inclusion of brief quotations in a review.

ISBN: 978-0-9897804-0-7

Copyright © 2013 by Douglas Mong & James Tintle
First Edition, 2013
Published in United States of America

ColdBlooded Publishing, LLC
P.O. Box 1671
Valrico, FL 33595

Disclaimer

Some images within this book have been "cleaned up" within Adobe Photoshop in order to correct imperfections within the picture. This was not done for the purpose of deception, but merely to provide a truer photographic representation of what these snakes should look like under ideal conditions. Thus, the occasional photograph imperfection has been cosmetically corrected via computer. My apologies to anyone who takes offense to such actions (I know there are "purists" in the reptile collecting community who object to picture modifications in any form), but I felt they added to the overall presentation of the book, and showed true and correct coloration of the snakes provided.

Unless otherwise noted all pictures within this book are copyrighted to Douglas Mong or James Tintle. Except where noted all pictures are exclusive property of either the named individuals providing the pictures, Douglas Mong, James Tintle, or Coldblooded Publishing, Inc. These images may not be reproduced, copied, transmitted, and/or modified without the written consent of the exclusive owner(s).

This book is designed to provide information on Honduran Milksnakes, Lampropeltis triangulum hondurensis only. This information is provided and sold with the knowledge that the publisher and author do not offer any legal or other professional advice. In the case of a need for any such expertise consult with the appropriate professional. This book does not contain all information available on the subject. This book has not been created to be specific to any individual's or organizations' situation or needs. Every effort has been made to make this book as accurate as possible. However, there may be typographical and or content errors. Therefore, this book should serve only as a general guide and not as the ultimate source of subject information. This book contains information that might be dated and is intended only to educate and entertain. The author and publisher shall have no liability or responsibility to any person or entity regarding any loss or damage incurred, or alleged to have incurred, directly or indirectly, by the information contained in this book. You hereby agree to be bound by this disclaimer or you may return this book within 90 days from date of purchase for a full refund.

Dedication

It is with great admiration and respect that the authors wish to dedicate this book to two very renowned herpetologists that have passed away recently; Bill Haast, and Joseph T. Collins. These herpetologists blazed a trail that helped forge what our wonderful snake hobby is today. What they have contributed to herpetology and science are legacies that will live on forever...........

Bill Haast (December 30, 1910 - June 15, 2011)

Bill Haast is best known for his very extensive work and research with different types of snake venom. In 1946 after WWII, Bill and his son started a few small buildings and outside exhibit that would later gradually transform into the famous landmark facility known as the Miami Serpentarium. It was here that Bill conducted his research and many venom extractions. Aside from the private laboratory, it also housed countless types of snakes, both venomous and non-venomous for the general public to see first-hand. Visitors could also experience his famous King Cobra shows held out on the large open lawn where Haast would either tube feed or extract the venom of very large King Cobra specimens. Mr. Haast also published an autobiography of his interesting life called "Cobras in His Garden".

Along with his monumental involvement with venom for the medical field, his famous Serpentarium was undoubtedly a key source that spawned early interest in snake keeping for many hobbyists and herpetoculturists alike over the years.

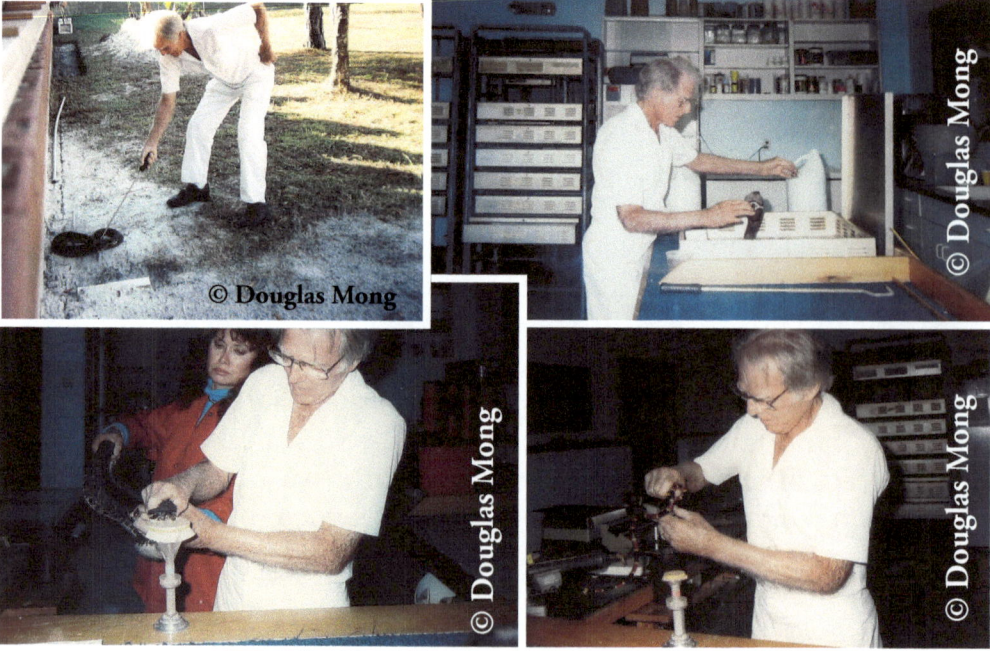

Photos provided Larry Miller of Kansas Heritage Photography

Joseph T. Collins (July 3, 1939 - January 14, 2012)

Joseph wrote his first scientific paper in 1959 and his first book in 1974. Since then, he has written over 300 scientific or semi-popular articles and 28 books. He served the OHS/SSAR for over 40 years as an Editor, Secretary, Committee chair, and as its President in 1978. In 1967 Joe joined the Museum of Natural History at the University of Kansas as a collections manager. He ultimately became the Editor of the Museums publications until his retirement on September, 5 1997 following a distinguished 30-year career. Notable achievements while at KU included his recognition as Conservationist of the Year by the Kansas Wildlife Federation, President of the Kansas Academy of Science, and the 1979 Classified Employee of the Year at KU. He and his wife, Suzanne later founded The Center for North American Herpetology (CNAH) in 1994. Mr. Collins was noted as being the most prolific author of the state of Kansas' wildlife, and he even co-authored the well-known Peterson Field Guide to Reptiles and Amphibians of Eastern and Central North America. All the while also being deeply involved with field work and teaching countless others about the Kansas areas wildlife and ecology. This dedicated herpetologist has certainly left quite an extensive foot-print so that others, as well as the animals themselves he cared so deeply about could greatly benefit in the future.

Foreword

Until 1998, when I hatched the world's first snow Honduran Milk Snake, breeders didn't even know if it could be done. Would the anerythristic and amelanistic genes reside in different places on an animal's chromosomes, so that both could exist on the same snake--making it possible to produce an animal that showed both traits? There were many other questions: How best to feed for optimum growth? What is "optimum" growth? How best to brumate to get the best breeding results? What tricks might encourage reluctant hatchlings to take their first meals? There was so much to learn.

Smart breeders had had successes and failures before me: Ernie Wagner, David Doherty, Brian Barczyk, Louis Porras and Bill and Kathy Love were pioneers. Still, we and an increasing number of others in the U.S. and abroad were on a ship with no map. And then we bumped into an imposing shoal: Were these animals even truly Honduran milksnakes?

On this entire journey Doug Mong was one of the most prolific contributors to our understanding, especially, but not just, in addressing the question of the animals' identity. Doug became the go-to guy on forums and at reptile expos for those wanting to know where these animals came from, how they got here, what they look like in their home range and how we distinguish them from the other Central American Milk Snakes. He excelled as both archivist and keeper. Jimmy Tintle combined his knowledge of the subspecies' natural history with keeping methods and pressed on locations, meristics, resolving misunderstandings and fighting misinformation.

Now their formidable knowledge is assembled in this book, providing answers that would have steered so many, so well, 15 years ago. They'll do no less for the huge numbers of Honduran keepers today. It's a project that's long overdue, and a project that lives up to its challenge.

~ Terry Dunham

Acknowledgements

It is with great gratitude that we, Douglas Mong & James Tintle wish to express thanks to those that have spent countless hours with us either conversing by telephone, email, and/or in person. Many of whom have provided personal pictures of animals needed in the completion of this book. We would especially like to thank:

Scott Ballard, Breck Bartholomew, Ric Blair, Shannon Brown, Paula Cummings, Dell Despain, Dave Doherty, Terry Dunham, Mike Falcon, Gerry Godin, Rusty Green, Cole Grover, Rich Goldzung, John Lambert, Neil Little, Jonel Lopez, Bill and Kathy Love, Terry Maheuron, Steve Michaels, Larry Miller, Dave Niles, Steve Osborne, Daniel Parker, Louis W. Porras, Dan Rieck, Peter Rice, Wayne Sanders, Robert Seib, Don and Sally Shores, Jorge Sierra, Tim Spuckler, Thomas Steffen, Stu Tennyson, Molli Thibodeaux, Ernie Wagner, Nathan Wells and Randy Whittington.

In addition to those mentioned above, we would also like to give a huge thanks to the many people (both past and present) that have contributed to the popularity of the Honduran milksnake hobby in its entirety over the years. It would be absolutely impossible to list all of the individuals that have ever worked with, or contributed to the popularity of these magnificent milksnakes, but here are some of them that certainly have…….

In alphabetical order:

Lee Abbott, Jeff Alloway, Michael Alvarez, Bob Applegate, Marc Bailey, Johnnie Ballentine, Brian and Lori Barczyk, Dave and Tracy Barker, Byron Barnes, Richard D. and Patricia Bartlett, Doug Beard, Mark and Kim Bell, Russ Bezette, Bill Brant, Kim Caldwell, Vaclav Chadima, John Cherry, Guy Clark, Deon and Kristen Collins, Tom Crutchfield, Dennis and Eric Daley, Norm Damm, Joe Exposito, John Fraser, Chad Fuchs, Tim Gebhard, Wes Greene, Dan Grubb, Rob Haneisen, Kevin Hanley, Tom Harbin, Gerrit Helming, Holger and Gabriele Hortenbach, Eric Hou, Dan Johnson, Rodney Jtineant, Jim and Helen Kavney, Gary Keasler, Jim Keenan, Mark Kenderdine, Karl Krumke, Hans Koenig, Jaap Kooij, Lenny Krysko, Matt Lackemeyer, Bill Lamar, Lloyd Lemke, Mark Lucas, Vinny Lynch, Jim Mabe, Rob MacInnes, Scott MacLeod, John Manser, Ronald G. Markel, Scott Melton, John Meltzer, Frank Menser, John Michaels, Bob Montoya, Greg Moss, Sean Niland, Regis Opferman, Brandon Osborne, Lance Portal, Lindsay Pike, Dwayne Richard, Bob Roth, Jon Roylance, Anthony Rufolo, Matt Salyer, Jim Sargent, John Schmitt, Charlie Shanklin, Brian Sharp, Ben Siegel, Chris Shulse, Tom Sierra, Bob Sligh, Don Soderberg, Rob and Louise Stevens, Tom Stevens, Don Stipp, Steve Strasser, Jeff Teel, Ted Thompson, Craig Tillem, Luis Torres, Rick Trenny, Terry Walters, Paul Weaver, and Kenneth L. Williams.

Contents

Disclaimer v
Dedication vi
Foreword viii
Acknowledgements ix
About the Authors xii
Introduction 2
The Early Years 5

Chapter 1
Hondurans in Captivity 10
Housing 11
 Substrate 16
Heating 17
Feeding 19

Chapter 2
Purchasing a Honduran Milksnake 28
Handling Your Recent Purchase 33

Chapter 3
Seasonal Changes & Breeding 36
Brumation 38
Spring Warm Up and Resuming Feeding 39
Courtship and Breeding Behavior 40
Egg-Laying and Incubation 42
Sexing Hatchlings 53

Chapter 4
Genetics 54

Chapter 5
Single Genetic Mutations 64
Amelanistic 65
Anerythristic 72
Hypomelanistic 80

Chapter 6
Double Genetic Mutations 90
Ghost 90
Hybino 97
Snow 99

Chapter 7
- Triple Genetic Mutations 102
- Pearl 103

Chapter 8
- Line-Bred Mutations 106
- Bailey Line 108
- Guy Clark "Crazy Line" 109
- European Line, aka Jaap Kooij Line 111
- Pin-banded 115
- Vanishing pattern 117
- Patternless..117
- Reverse Pattern..118
- Striped Aberrant 120
- Calico 121
- Burgundy 121
- Two-Headed (bicephalic) 122

Chapter 9
- Record Keeping 124

Chapter 10
- Taxonomy 128
- Meristics 130
- Anatomy 133

Chapter 11
- Distribution 136

Chapter 12
- Common Diseases and Illnesses..142
- Internal Parasites: (endoparasites) 146
- External Parasites: (ectoparasites) 148

Glossary 154
Breeders & Other Resources 158
Index 166

About the Authors

My deep passion for snakes started back in 1966-67 when I was only six or seven years old. Since that time of capturing my very first Rough Green Snake (Opheodrys aestivus) I have hunted and collected many different types of snakes ever since. Luckily for me, I had great parents that promoted my new found interest in these very special creatures. My mom would even buy me snakes for birthday's and Christmas' from a friend's husband who was an avid field collector down in southern Miami/Dade county where snakes were very abundant.

Later on when I started going to local reptile shows in south Florida around 1989 and beyond, I was like the proverbial kid in a candy store and found myself especially attracted to the colorful milksnakes that were available. After all, these were some of the gorgeous snakes that I drooled over that were depicted in several of the snake books I had growing up, and that I would dream of owning someday. As a young kid when I saw my very first Scarlet kingsnake in an older kid's aquarium that lived the next block over from me, I instantly knew that these would be some of the snakes that would grace my collection later on. Since those times decades ago, I have been learning and studying as much as I possibly could about milksnakes and many others. I have kept many different kinds of snakes over the years, but the genus Lampropeltis is most certainly one of my all-time favorites to have in my collection and work with.

Today, there are more types of snakes available to the hobbyist than ever before, as well as countless genetic mutations and multi-morph combinations. I have personally been breeding and producing snakes for about the past twenty-five years now, and ha found it very rewarding to selectively-breed some of the top-quality animals that

are in my small, modest collection. I can never seem to get enough, and continue learning, studying and researching as much as possible about them. Indeed, my life has revolved around snakes ever since I can remember, and I wouldn't give it up for the world...

~Douglas Mong

It was a warm summer afternoon during 1982. I was playing outside when I suddenly realized that the family dog was playing with an Eastern Box Turtle (Terrapene carolina carolina). I ran over to the dog to stop him from biting and chewing on this poor turtle. This was the moment that I realized that the cold-blooded creatures that were so poorly known by the common individual, were going to be much more than a sight to see. After saving the turtle from the dog, I ran inside to show my parents and to ask if I could keep it. Like most parents at that time there was a huge misunderstanding of the reptile world. No sooner than words were coming out of my mouth I heard two voices saying "No!" Over the next few years I searched the neighborhood not only for box turtles, but also found that snakes were more interesting to me.

A few years later, while visiting my grandparents, I found a ball of baby garter snakes up against the old water well. My grandmother knowing my enthusiasm with snakes came out and helped me collect a bucket full of the baby snakes. Once again, the answer was no to keeping them. After years of searching and finding snakes in the wild, I was finally old enough to be able to care for the snakes on my own.

In 1994, I bought my first snake, like most of us it was a corn snake (Pantherophis guttatus guttatus). It was only a short time later that the collection grew to a few more, but this time they were color mutations. Milksnakes came into my life a year or so later when I finally went to a local trade show, where the pictures I had only seen in books and magazines finally came to life. I purchased my first pair of Mexican Milksnakes (Lampropeltis triangulum annulata) at that show, and my interests with the various species of the genus Lampropeltis have never stopped.

~James Tintle

Louis Porras holding a gigantic tangerine *L.t.hondurensis* imported from "The Shed" in Miami, Florida in the late 1970s. This animal was later sold too Zooherp (background) in the mid- 1990s. This specimen measured an incredible 7'-11" long!

Introduction

With the explosive popularity of snakes as pets in more recent years, and the never ending increase of people enjoying the outdoors, more people have encountered snakes in the wild. This would often lead to the interest of keeping them for many once the idea was kindled. Today there are more pet stores that carry reptiles than ever before. They can often be found as you walk through local malls, as well as see large assortments of reptiles on the vast array of internet sites online. They can also be easily accessed on many reptile forums, reptile classified ads, and different reptile shows around the country.

All of this combined has led to their being far more popular in recent years. Television nature shows have also made people more aware of these interesting creatures, even though they aren't always portrayed in a positive light. This of course is for the general public's viewing drama and "wow" factor. These are just a few of the leading reasons for the increased popularity of snakes we see today.

Milksnakes (*Lampropeltis triangulum*), and other tri-colored kingsnakes belong to a group of snakes that mimic Coral Snakes. This means they resemble Coral Snakes in the three colors they display on their body. Though the three colors are the same, the color sequence of the rings are very different between the two, as are the more blunt and rounded snout structure of the Coral Snakes. There is an old adage that goes....."Red touching black, venom lack; Red touching yellow, kill a fellow". This certainly applies to the typical races of Coral Snakes found in the U.S. However, be very aware that this rhyme DOES NOT always apply to some of the more obscure Central and South American forms of Coral Snakes in which the sequence of the rings do not always follow this general rule of thumb. The adage also doesn't apply to certain aberrant Eastern Coral Snakes (*Micrurus f.fulvius*).

Some of the aberrant specimens found in Monroe County in the upper Keys area over the years would not follow the adage.

Honduran milksnakes (*Lampropeltis triangulum hondurensis*) were first described by Kenneth L.Williams in 1978 when he released *Systematics and Natural History of the American Milk Snake, Lampropeltis triangulum; published by Milwaukee Public Museum*. Williams also described various other subspecies of milksnakes at this time, including *L.t.andesiana, L.t.conanti, L.t.sinaloae, L.t.smithi,* and *L.t.stuarti*. Williams revisited the complex in 1988 when he released the second edition of *Systematics and Natural History of the American Milksnake, Lampropeltis triangulum published by Milwaukee Public Museum*.

Decades ago, it was basically just a dream for people to own many of these gorgeous animals that were depicted in some of the older books we used to read growing up. Books like the ones written by Karl Kaufield, Raymond Ditmars, Roger Conant, Hobart Smith and others. Even the inexpensive pamphlet-type booklets that herpetologists and field workers like Ross Allen wrote about Florida's snakes were very exciting to read through and look at all the different photos. Finding snakes out in the wild wherever you lived in the country was plenty exciting, and about as good as it got when you came home with at least a snake or two in your pillowcase.

There were also dedicated people like the renowned Dr. Bernard Bechtel that pioneered and experimented with snake genetics very early-on. He acquired a wild-caught amelanistic (albino) cornsnake that was found in North Carolina back in 1953. He later bred this mutant snake to several wild-collected females in 1959. He then raised these babies up, and bred some of those normal-looking offspring to each other when they matured. These subsequent breedings proved the mode of inheritance to be recessive, thus producing the very first captive-bred amelanistics in 1961!

An interesting aberrant specimen collected from the San Pedro Sula area of northwestern Honduras

© **Louis W. Porras**

Breeding snakes wasn't much of a thought to most people that were interested in snakes back in those days, or even later for that matter. As time went on though, more and more people began to realize that they didn't have to depend solely on finding snakes themselves. Nor did they have to always locate some of the hard-to-find places that specialized in selling exotic animals to be able to enjoy more of these fascinating animals. Remember, this was many years ago and well before the technical advent of the internet. Some of these early breeding pioneers found that they could even make some fair income at the same time by either selling animals they collected, or the offspring that were produced. Since those days, the herpetocultural hobby has grown by leaps and bounds. Years later, Honduran Milksnakes have become some of the most widely available and bred milksnakes in the hobby after they started flowing into this country. When the first genetic mutations began to appear, it was definitely GAME ON!..........

The primary purpose of this book is for it to be the "one-stop" source to learn all about Honduran Milksnakes. Including their genetic mutations, multi-gene combinations, line-bred traits and their seemingly endless variations thereof. Throughout this book, you will also learn everything you need to know regarding their proper captive husbandry. Whether you're a casual hobbyist, or more advanced keeper, this information will help you accurately identify the many different color and pattern mutations, as well as their complete genetics from A to Z. It will also allow you to come to a more educated conclusion of whether the snake(s) you have, or are looking to purchase fall within this

A juvenile specimen collected from the San Pedro Sula area of Honduras near Henry Quin's compound.

© Louis W. Porras

colorful and often misidentified subspecies or not. Today there are many professional herpetoculturists and hobbyists alike attempting to breed for very specific looks, and it can often become quite confusing for the beginner.

As you read further on, you will also begin to get more familiar with some of the other very closely-related Central American subspecies. These snakes are also commonly misidentified and can often be a composite of the general "Hobby Hondurans" overall genetic makeup. Additionally, we will be referring to the "Hobby Hondurans" throughout this book unless otherwise stated. When referring to authentic specimens, Latin names will be used throughout the book (e.g. *L.t.hondurensis*).

The Early Years

Ever since the mid-late 1970s and 80s, countless milksnakes of several different subspecies from Central America have been imported into the United States and Europe. Many of which were collected and exported from different areas of Honduras. This also sometimes included subspecies on the Pacific slope side of Honduras, El Salvador, and other nearby adjacent areas. One has to keep in mind that during the course of all this, the individual field collectors of these wild specimens were certainly not milksnake identification experts. Nor were many of the exporters that boxed them, labeled them and marketed these snakes as they arrived here in the states. As a matter of fact, in that particular part of the world, these different types of milksnakes (*triangulum*) are simply known as "falsa, or falso coralillos" (False Coral Snakes).

Same impressive snake depicted in photograph on page 1.

The political influences and "red tape" that govern just about every other type of goods or commodities shipped and sold around the world surely had to also apply to many of these snake shipments too. Where some of these snakes ended up being shipped from didn't necessarily mean this was where they were actually collected, and vice-versa. When the U.S. importers obtained these snakes, they tended to sort them out and disperse them to dealers according to whatever best suited their marketability, or whatever they figured the snakes tended to best represent. Additionally, even at their final store destination, some were likely looked at and "renamed" according to what the store operator may have figured they were.

When you consider all this, it isn't very realistic to think that all of these snakes continuously being imported were necessarily 100% authentic subspecies in their "purest" form. Although, a large number of them certainly were. Many of these were "pure" genuine forms of *L.t.hondurensis* from the interior of their large range. Others were likely some of the other neighboring subspecies or intergrade forms as well. The very same scenario would also apply to the other "pure" forms of similar looking Central American subspecies native to those general areas that were shipped in over the years. These other types brought in would include *L.t.abnorma*, *L.t.polyzona*, *L.t.stuarti* and *L.t.oligozona*. Other triangulum that are native to Mexico and further down into Central and South America that have been imported into the pet trade can often be misidentified just the same.

Even after all the above is considered, you also have to understand that the huge numbers of casual hobbyists that have bred all of these different milksnakes over the years didn't really understand how to distinguish between them either. Most didn't know where they came from at all, and could only go by what they were told they were and labeled as by others. These hobbyists basically bred them with whatever subspecies they thought they probably had in their collections at any given time. To the average hobbyist, just about any Central American milksnake with multi-colored rings and a snout band would basically seem like a "Honduran" Milksnake. After all, this is the subspecies most everyone in the hobby has been familiar with hearing about all this time. Still to this day,

This very odd looking and unique hypo *L.t.hondurensis* was collected in eastern Nicaragua.

© Louis W. Porras

most hobbyists have a very difficult time distinguishing the specific differences between these snakes. Even well-seasoned milksnake breeders aren't very familiar with identifying the subtle differences of these snakes.

To toss a wrench into the confusing matter even further, there isn't a single Kingsnake-Milksnake book on the entire market that doesn't have at least a couple misidentified photographs depicting some of these subspecies. More than a few have struggled to try and learn how to accurately identify these snakes and their true ranges over the years, but more often than not they were left less than uncertain. They found that this was far easier said than done once they started researching into this in more depth. The truth of the matter is that most of the books only made some of these identifications even more confusing.

Some of the first Guatemalan Milksnakes (*L.t.abnorma*) that were imported into the states in the mid-late 1980s originating from Lago de Izabal are just one prime example of the previous scenarios mentioned. By the time a fair number of these were later produced by others, they too eventually got mixed into the hobby Honduran genetic "melting pot" and totally disappeared from the hobby altogether in only the mid-late 90s. It wasn't until just very recently when a few authentic imports surfaced and were produced once again in very limited numbers.

A "Tangerine Dream" from Bill Love's stock that Louie Porras acquired in the 1990s.

© Louis W. Porras

Needless to say, this is all precisely why the visual characteristics of some of the other similar looking subspecies such as *L.t.polyzona*, *L.t.stuarti*, and even *L.t.oligozona* and *L.t.abnorma* can sometimes be seen in today's "Hobby Honduran" milksnakes.

Now that some of the basic problematic history of the Honduran Milksnakes and the other similar looking subspecies is better understood, you can begin to see just how this all evolved. Many of the Honduran Milksnakes in today's hobby do "key-out" meristically as *L.t.hondurensis*. The fact is, a substantial amount of them can consist of varying percentages of some of the other Central American subspecies. Logically, some have less intergrade influence than others, and even some possibly have none at all. The real question would be; how would you ever know? This all depends on what their past locale origins were to begin with, and what they were actually bred with over the years. As mentioned before, hardly anyone has kept any of the true *L.t.hondurensis* bloodlines just as they originally were from the very start. This is exactly how the dynamics of most of the other species in the hobby works too. Most breeders today are more concerned with mixing things to create different looking variations than they are with preserving certain subspecies or bloodlines. There's certainly nothing wrong with producing interesting looking snakes, but the other side to this is that some of the specific bloodlines, or even authentic subspecies could instantly terminate in the process.

Today, there are only a few truly authentic *L.t.hondurensis* bloodlines known to exist in private captive collections. It is basically the very same thing regarding several of the other Central American milksnake subspecies. These other, less commonly seen races are also extremely few and far between in their "pure" form. This is also due to the very same misidentification and inadvertent breedings that have taken place over the years.

It takes quite a bit of knowledge, experience and dedicated research to accurately identify some of these different milksnakes. All of this is far more than the casual milksnake hobbyist is usually willing to dedicate themselves to. It is also extremely important to realize that without corresponding locality data from their true place of origin, all one can go by is their outward visual phenotype. When all is said and done, the "Hobby Hondurans" are what they are because of the decades of different bloodlines and countless generations of captive-breedings.

(Top) High-black normal
(Middle) High-black anerythristic
(Bottom) High-white amelanistic

A Collective History of Honduran Milksnakes for the Hobbyist

Chapter 1
Hondurans in Captivity

© Gerry Godin

Honduran Milksnakes have been the main stage for many breakthrough advances in captive snake keeping. Their ease of care, impressive size, and their willingness to reproduce in captivity has made them one of the most popular of all the milksnakes. There are many ways to keep Honduran Milksnakes in captivity, and there are a few basic necessities needed for them to thrive.

Housing

The housing quarters for Hondurans can be very basic, or as elaborate as the keeper wants. This depends on if the individual enclosures are for larger numbers of snakes for convenience (e.g. rack systems), or if the keeper wants a more visually pleasing setup for just one or two snakes to display in separate vivariums.

Housing Hatchling Milksnakes

Hatchlings do best when started in small containers. Never under *any* circumstances, should hatchlings be housed in the same container, as this can run great risk of cannibalism. The only exception to this is when they are fresh hatchlings leaving the eggs, and are still full of belly yolk. Hatchling and juvenile milksnakes are naturally very nervous to begin with, and feel far more vulnerable to predators than older, larger snakes would. Being out in the open and vulnerable is the last thing in the world a tiny milksnake would ever want to do in the wild. The only exception to this would be for foraging during the cover of night, and it is really just the same in captivity. Hatchlings and juveniles can easily be setup in small shoebox sized plastic containers that have tiny holes drilled or melted in them to allow sufficient air circulation. This is easily done with a small drill bit, or very inexpensive 1/8th" soldering gun tip.

The lids MUST be well-fitted and very secure to prevent escapes. Milksnakes are among the best escape artists on the planet. It cannot be stressed enough that almost everyone that has ever kept snakes for any real length of time has likely had a snake or two escape from underestimating their ability to do so.

➔ Housing
➔ Heat
➔ Water
➔ Food

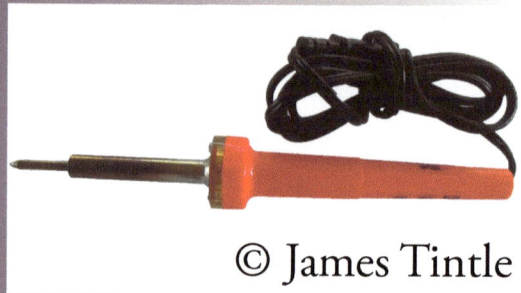
© James Tintle

© Reptile Basics

A low-profile small hide box, or even a plastic coffee lid or other small container with a small notch cut out of the side works great for hides. A dark color also works best, because the color "black" in nature means cover and shadows to hide in to a snake. Snakes are hard-wired for searching out dark places to hide. A fairly "snug" fitting hide seems to work best for allowing milksnakes to feel secure. This is extremely important, especially for smaller, younger milksnakes that aren't accustomed to captivity as the larger, older milksnakes are.

Milksnakes should be kept dry, but they also need a certain amount of humidity to keep from dehydrating and to help facilitate with shedding their skin (ecdysis). This can either be done by having an adjustable humidifier placed in the snake room, or by simply placing what's known as a "humid hide" in the enclosure with them. Most people choose to use the very inexpensive containers that they have lying around the house to fashion these out of. These can be made out of simple household plastic containers filled with moist sphagnum moss with an entry notch cut into the lid or side. Typically, a relative humidity of around 50 percent or more allows them to shed successfully. This is especially important in the fall and winter months when the air is naturally much drier, and from it being heated from a furnace or other type of A/C unit.

© Gerry Godin

Shedding and Growth Rate

After hatchlings have shed for the very first time and have begun eating on a reliable schedule, they will begin growing at a phenomenal rate. As they grow, they will shed their outer skin periodically. A snake's skin isn't like many other animals that will constantly slough off as it grows, or molt in many pieces like lizards do. The scales underneath the old surface layer will grow to a certain point, and then be replaced by the newly developed scale layer from underneath, and so on. If the young snakes are fed well, every three to five days, they can be expected to undergo a shed every several weeks. They will continue to do this throughout their entire lives according to how much they eat and grow at any given time. In nature, as well as captivity, this will all depend on the seasons, temperatures, frequency and size of the meals they consume.

© Douglas Mong

The snakes eyes and overall body appearance will look very cloudy and dull compared to how it does normally. After noticing the change in coloration, the snake will clear up somewhat within 5-7 days. At this time the snake will still have a lackluster appearance. Two to five days after the eye lenses clear, the snake will then shed. They generally shed in one continuous piece. Often it can get broken off in smaller pieces as they crawl and rub against object surfaces within the enclosure, and even back and forth against themselves in odd directions. It is *EXTREMELY* important to make sure once they shed that the entire shed comes completely off. It is especially important to check that the clear eye cap lenses (brille) both come off, as well as the tail tip.

If these things are overlooked and are allowed to stay on the snake, this can lead

A close-up view of a nice custom-built vivarium setup that Gerry Godin built. An expanded view of the same vivarium setup on the opposite page.

© Gerry Godin

Commercially built plastic hide boxes or even home made hide boxes are very important to your newly acquired Honduran Milksnake. (Courtesy of Reptile Basics)

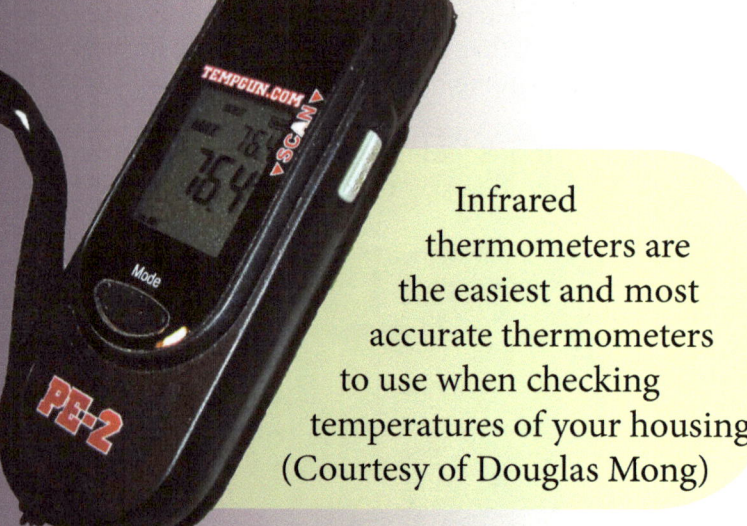

Infrared thermometers are the easiest and most accurate thermometers to use when checking temperatures of your housing. (Courtesy of Douglas Mong)

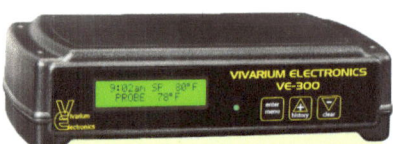

Electronic controlled thermostat for heating elements. Use of this type of product is recommended when using heat tapes, heat cables, heat pads and any other heating elements. (Courtesy of Reptile Basics)

Flexwatt heat tape is one of the most commonly used type of heating elements for Honduran Milksnakes, It can be used for various forms of housing applicaations. (Courtesy of Reptile Basics)

A simple juvenile setup made out of a small shoebox, small plastic flower pot and water bowl.

snakes might "seem" like they stopped growing altogether when they are full-grown adults, especially when you are so used to seeing them all the time. If you could literally stretch them fully out and measure them to the smallest fraction of an inch, over time you would find that they always continue to grow. Milksnakes can live for a very long time, and they can typically live anywhere from 15-20 years, and sometimes longer.

Housing Subadults and Adults

to other serious health issues. The eyes can become infected from underneath if this goes on for an extended amount of time. They can even go blind when other sheds compound on top of the older one(s) to make things worse. If the shed skin on the tip of the tail doesn't come off completely, it can tighten as it dries and shrinks, constricting the blood flow to the tip and can eventually die and fall off.

As your snake gradually becomes larger, they can be moved accordingly to bigger enclosures. Most adult Honduran Milksnakes can be kept adequately in well-ventilated large plastic sweater boxes. These are typically housed in a rack system. These systems can be either homemade or company-bought for convenience and ease of feeding and maintenance. When the snake collection becomes larger, these rack systems work well. These are typically built with either expanded PVC, or with metal tubing, depending on your specific needs and personal preference. Most commercial rack systems are heated by Flexwatt heat tape or heat cable. You must use a thermostat with these types of heating elements, or you can easily overheat the enclosure. Alternatively, snakes can also be kept in other caging and vivarium-type setups.

Very opaque Extreme Hypo in "full-blue" going into a shed cycle.

Some snakes will refuse to feed at this time, while some will reluctantly feed (often only on smaller than normal prey items). Regardless, all will resume their normal feeding schedule after they successfully shed.

Snakes grow at their fastest rate in the first two years of life. They will gradually slow down as they continue to age. Older

© James Tintle

Aspen Shavings, Aspen Chips, and Coconut Coir

Substrate

There are several choices available to the keeper when it comes to choosing substrate. Newspaper, coconut bark and aspen are just a few. The authors have been using shredded aspen for almost all of their snakes for many years. The reasons being, it is very absorbent and easy to spot-clean until the entire substrate is changed out.

Over the years there has been much debate over whether pine shavings are an acceptable substrate for reptiles. Due to the close similarity it has to cedar shavings, pine shavings could possibly carry the same ill effects to your snake as cedar can. The extracts from softwoods like pine and cedar contain various aromatic compounds including hydrocarbons. Naphthalene, the active ingredient in mothballs has also been found in these shavings.

Most of the research on the effects of using cedar and pine shavings has been done in warm-blooded animals, for example, rodents and birds. Research has shown significant evidence that the hydrocarbons breakdown the cell walls of the lungs. This has been known to cause respiratory infections and opens areas for possible secondary infections.

Besides the inevitable respiratory infections, there have been reports that show enlarged livers on warm blooded animals that were kept on cedar and pine shavings. These are very hard to detect from the outside looking at an animal, and typically can only be discovered after a necropsy of the deceased animal is performed. Just imagine the effects on your captive milksnake that does a lot of burrowing and hiding within these shavings. The snakes would be in greater threat as their bodies are surrounded by the fumes and the oils, as they are leached directly into the skin and mucous membranes.

Even with the great success of many veteran breeders using pine shavings for many years, it is your choice as a responsible reptile keeper to make an educated choice of substrates. There are enough products available now that have shown no known adverse effects on captive milksnakes.

Many people like to keep the theme of materials used to correspond with the basic natural habitat that a particular snake comes from in the wild. In the case with Honduran Milksnakes, this could be a mulch bedding bought from the garden area of your local department store or home center. If you choose to use a product such as garden mulch, be sure it has been heat-treated prior to the snake being placed inside with it. This greatly reduces the likelihood of any unwanted insects or organisms. There are also many companies that offer pre-treated and kiln-dried bark substrates for reptiles. The only real drawback to using these dark colored materials is that the snake feces are not as easy to see. If you don't own too many snakes, then this might not be an issue at all, and could be a great option to consider.

Milksnakes are generally terrestrial (ground-dwelling) snakes, and are not particularly known for their arboreal climbing abilities. However, a nice decorative climbing branch can be added for aesthetics. They will certainly use it from time to time as they carry out their routine daily activity. It is recommended to purchase your decorative material from pet shops or other reptile suppliers, as these are typically treated.

Heating

Providing heat for a portion of your snake enclosures can be done in various ways. Some of the commercial heat mats, heat tapes, or heat cables designed for reptile usage are a preferred way of heating them. Stay away from incandescent light bulbs and ceramic heat emitters, as these will tend to dry your snakes out and can be dangerous to the snake, especially if it comes in contact with them. Thermostats, rheostats or other components help prevent any drastic temperature fluctuations, and to keep the heat source as fail-safe as possible. These items can easily be found for sale online or at other reptile suppliers. Many rack systems are sold with the option of having heat tape already installed. They also come with thermostats to fit the individual's budget and needs.

Just always keep in mind, whatever method you choose to use for heating your snakes enclosure, monitor the temperatures very closely for at least a full 24 hr. period. During this time, you have a chance to tweak and fine-tune it as necessary BEFORE you put the snake in.

The important thing to remember about heating the warm side of the enclosure is it has to be closely monitored. Temperatures should be taken at the enclosures actual floor surface where the snake's belly will make contact. This way you know exactly what the warmest temperature is within the enclosure. For the cooler side, the ambient air temp reading towards the bottom where the snake will be works fine. Also, if the substrate is placed in thick enough, this also allows for an additional temperature gradient that the snake can utilize. The snake will dig lower down to seek the warmer temperatures, and anywhere in between the floor and top surface of the substrate for any given situation.

© Rusty Green

Honduran Milksnakes do best when provided a temperate gradient between 75F and 88-90F. In order to achieve these optimum temperatures your snakes caging needs to be of adequate size. You will notice your snake utilizing the warmer end of the cage after a recently consumed prey item. This allows them to properly digest their meal. In order to conserve energy in between, the snake will typically move to the cooler end to achieve this.

Water Requirements

The water bowl needs to be large enough for the snake to soak in without spilling over the edge and soaking the substrate. The snakes may soak in the water bowl for various reasons, but most notably for hydrating their skin just prior to ecdysis, the process of shedding the skin. Make sure your snakes have fresh water at all times. Change it immediately if there are any feces or urates in the bowl. Not doing this will promote serious disease and infections.

Mega ghost and Mega hypomelanistic Honduran Milksnake.

Other times they might choose to soak in the water bowl if the temperatures are too high, or if they have mites. So it is very important to keep close tabs on your snakes periodically to see if there are any changes in their behavior or environment that need to be addressed. Mites and other parasites will be covered in chapter 12.

Feeding

Live vs. Frozen

There are two choices to consider regarding the rodents your snakes will be fed. One option is to raise your own; the other is buying pre-killed frozen rodents. There are many dedicated companies offering frozen rodents online too.

© Gerry Godin

Tricolor L.t.hondurensis originating from parents imported from central Nicaragua.

© Shannon Brown

Herpetological societies can provide you with local rodent breeders, and reptile magazines and forums are great resources as well.

Live

Many snake keepers will opt to raise their own rodents by keeping one male and multiple females in a breeding bin. With raising live prey, it can be very convenient to go gather up the number of rodents you need for however many snakes you want to feed. With raising your own rodents you can freeze the surplus that you don't use. This can be very handy when the mice are at certain sizes so they will not get larger than what is required for your snake's particular size.

Some of the down-sides of raising your own rodents might be the odor. If the containers are cleaned on a well-managed schedule the odor won't be a big issue, especially if you only own a few snakes. There are also many air purifying machines on the market that help immensely with controlling odor. Another thing to consider would be the cost of rodent chow and bedding for the breeding colonies. The time to do all this efficiently is of course just one more thing you would need to consider. These will all be important factors regarding what the best choice is for any individual keeper.

Frozen

Buying frozen rodents are a fantastic option for those that don't wish to raise their own rodent supply. As mentioned previously, there are many companies that you can buy pre-packaged rodents from. They come in every size for any snake(s) you may happen to have. The sizes range from small pinkies, large pinkies, peach fuzzies, fuzzies, hoppers, weanlings, adult mice and extra-large/jumbo mice. Rats can be bought from these companies in all these various sizes too, as well as chicks if you want to add some variety for your adult snakes.

Many folks (including the authors) choose to buy frozen rodents for their snakes. With frozen rodents there is no unpleasant odor to deal with, nor is there any maintenance involved. You simply take out the appropriately marked bag that coincides with the size of the snakes that are to be fed, then return the bag to the freezer. The method of freezing the rodents also greatly reduces the risk of parasites and disease being transferred either to you or your snakes. Another great thing about frozen rodents is that it kills

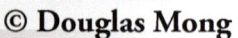
© Douglas Mong

many parasites that feed internally on the prey host.

Honduran Milksnakes will typically do very well on a diet of mice alone. However, when the snakes become larger you may want to consider feeding rats instead of mice. A small rat generally costs about the same as two large mice. It is definitely cheaper if it takes three larger mice to equal the same mass as an appropriately sized rat. When the keeper has many mouths to feed, the option of feeding rats to larger snakes can be less time consuming, less expensive, and just plain more convenient. Also, rats typically have larger heads and a bigger bone structure which would likely allow for more calcium intake. Newborn rat pinkies and rat pups can be fed to the smaller snakes too, so the choice is there to either feed mice or rats to just about any sized snake you happen to have except for the very smallest juveniles.

Mice vs. Rats

Some Hondurans, as well as many other types of snakes can have an individual preference for one or the other type of rodent. There are many times when a keeper offers a snake a rat that has always been fed mice, and they don't seem to like the scent of the rat and refuse to eat it. By the same token, it can work the other way around too, and rat feeders may not want anything to do with a mouse that is offered. If either of these situations happen, and you only have one type of food available at the moment until you can get another supply of the preferred prey items, there are some scenting techniques that can often work.

One method is to simply put the desired prey item in with the other source that you want the snake to eat. If you are raising live rodents, you can get a big scoop of the used bedding substrate from the bin of desired type of rodents you are raising. Then put the used shavings in a separate container with the other type of rodent the snake doesn't want to accept. This helps transfer the preferred scent over to the desired prey item. If you are using frozen rodents, you can put one or two of the prey items in a big bag of the other rodents for a while to transfer the scent over to those.

If this doesn't seem to work, you can try piercing the nose, or slicing the skull (braining) either the rat or mouse and gently squeeze and smear the brain material onto the face and snout of the desired prey item. It is best to make sure that you offer the now scented meal head first to the snake so it only smells the face that was intentionally scented. A long set of tongs works great for introducing thawed prey directly in front of the face of the snake.

BABY'S FIRST MEAL

1. Offer a frozen thawed pinkie at the entrance of their hide. Typically this will work, if not go to step 2.

2. Offer a frozen thawed pinkie but tear the nose off to expose the tissue underneath the skin. If refused go to step 3.

3. Offer a live pinkie overnight inside of the snake's enclosure. If refused go to step 4.

4. Offer a brained frozen thawed pinkie. This is not for the faint of heart as this procedure involves slicing the pinkie from snout to top of head with a razor blade. Offer these in a small deli cup and place back inside the enclosure overnight. If refused go to step 5.

5. Continue steps 1-4 at 3 day intervals until the snake has consumed its first meal. If the snake is still refusing to eat after a couple of months, there are a few alternative steps. These include scenting, tease feeding and eventually force feeding. The former are last resort efforts to getting baby snakes to eat.

Feeding hatchlings

Feeding baby Honduran Milksnakes is pretty straight-forward. Hatchlings are generally good about accepting pinkies (newborn mice) right from the start. This is one more reason that they are so popular in today's hobby. Baby snakes are born with a substantial yolk reserve that gives them a good head start on life in the wild until their feeding response develops and can begin to locate prey.

After they hatch, it generally takes somewhere between eight and twelve days for them to undergo their first shed. Some hatchlings will accept food prior to this first shed. The authors personally like to wait until well after they shed to offer food for the first time. This is so they are good and hungry first, and that their yolk reserves have started to become a bit more depleted.

A hatchling snake can go quite a long time, weeks sometimes even months without food. However, finding out just how long they can go is definitely not something you want them or yourself to have to go through. You certainly don't want them to go months without feeding, but they sometimes can before their body reserves become completely exhausted.

It is extremely important that you get them to feed before it becomes a major issue later in the game with doing whatever is needed. This might include some of the scenting tricks mentioned earlier, as well as more techniques and tips further on in this chapter. The first thing that needs to be considered in order for them to eat and digest properly is optimum temperatures. They need to have enough warmth to digest their food properly to prevent regurgitation. The procedures for this need to be carefully followed as mentioned in the "heating" section described earlier in this chapter.

If an optimum temperature gradient cannot be achieved for whatever reason(s), a static temperature in their small enclosure of the low to mid 80s during the day, dropping slightly at night can work reasonably well. But this is really a marginal way of husbandry compared to them having a wider range of temperatures to utilize.

The first meal for a hatchling should be small enough that it can be easily swallowed. If it is too large, and they eventually give up and spit it out, this can sometimes discourage them from accepting their next offering. You want the rodent to be about the same size, or just slightly larger than the snake's head, and large enough to leave a visible bulge in the snake's mid-section when it goes down. When given ample belly heat for them to properly digest, hatchling Honduran Milksnakes will do very well when fed an appropriately sized rodent every three to five days. Obviously the more they are fed, the faster they will grow. Feeding them more than every three days may cause regurgitation and other major health issues.

After the snake has been in its enclosure for a while and has acclimated, offer the pinkie with a long set of thin tongs or hemostats. Generally, you will find the snake resting inside its hide box. If this is the case, offer the pinkie head-first at the entrance to the hide. Typically you will get a great ambush feeding response this way. This response is far more natural. A lot of breeders start hatchlings off feeding in small deli cups or other small containers. This keeps the hatchling and prey item in close proximity to each other. Most of the time, this technique will work if left in a dark quite place for several hours, or overnight.

© Rusty Green

It is a good idea to start out by trying to feed the hatchlings the type of prey you want them to be eating for the duration of their life. For many keepers, this would mean trying frozen/thawed first. However, live are absolutely fine if the keeper can supply them, or at least have access to them until they start accepting frozen thawed pinkies. If offering frozen/thawed does not seem to work after a few tries, giving a couple of days in between attempts, tearing the snout up well on a thawed-out pinkie can often work like magic. The scent of this freshly-torn body tissue seems to smell much more appealing to certain hatchlings.

The scenting technique known as "braining" is similar to the above snout tearing method. With this method you slice the head of the thawed pinkie open with a razor blade. Squeeze out some of the brain material and smear it liberally all over the head of the pinkie. Many times hatchlings that are reluctant to feed on a regular thawed pinkie, will find the scent of the moist brain material irresistible. For the next feeding offer a non-brained pinkie. If the hatchling does not accept this, continue with the braining technique, only applying a little less scenting each time. This way, they will gradually begin to associate the scent of a normal pinkie as their normal prey item.

Sometimes, although rare, the actual scent of the pinkies themselves can be a complete turn-off altogether for some reason, no matter how they are offered. For these snakes, you can try thoroughly rinsing, or even washing the pinkie well with an unscented soap. This trick can sometimes work surprisingly well for some reason.

Another technique that can be used with very stubborn hatchlings is a method called "tease-feeding". This involves gently grasping the hatchling behind the head, but not so firm that it feels totally restrained and allows some slight neck movement. Take the pinkie in your free hand and gently move the pinkie from side to side in a sort of gentle nudging or "slapping" motion against the hatchling's snout. Usually the snake will open its mouth and clamp down on the pinkie. If it does, this is when you DO NOT want to move at all or it will startle the snake and distract it from eating the pinkie and cause it to flee.

At this point you just want to hold it loosely enough to see if it will initiate its feeding instincts and continue swallowing the pinkie. If it does start to swallow, continue holding it just as you are until it has swallowed the pinkie all the way down. If they want to crawl forward with the pinkie in their mouth, you can gently and very slowly lower it down into a container so it can finish without being disturbed. Either way, the hatchling will need to be put back in its enclosure and left alone to digest the meal in peace.

Some of these exact same methods can be applied to feeding live prey items as well. One of the possibilities to feeding live prey items can sometimes be that the hatchling will become frightened of the pinkie being offered. If this is the case, using any of the aforementioned frozen thawed techniques may work better.

They key here is to not get discouraged and keep trying these different things every few days until they eventually develop a feeding response. The authors, as well as countless other keepers have done all of these things many times in the past. At some point, one of these methods always seems to work. It just takes some patience with certain snakes. The most important thing is to just stick with it and don't allow yourself to become discouraged.

© **Rusty Green**

Feeding sub-adults and adults

Feeding sub-adults and adult Honduran Milksnakes is generally much less involved because they have obviously already been feeding on their own for quite some time and are already well-established feeders. The important thing to keep in mind with larger, more mature snakes is to feed them enough

to keep a good optimum body weight, but not so much as to allow obesity. In captivity, your snake will not need to take advantage of every single feeding opportunity that it might in the wild. In nature it can often be a "feast or famine" situation and can greatly depend on the seasonal availability of the prey as well.

This is certainly not the case with your captive snake, so keeping an eye on their food intake and body weight becomes something you need to keep in mind as it gets more mature into adulthood. When the snakes are much younger and smaller, they will utilize their entire calorie intake for growing as fast as possible. Adults don't need as much calorie intake to maintain an optimal body weight. They only need to sustain their body mass. With adult females though, depending on if they are to be bred and produce eggs, this is a very different story. This will be discussed in more detail in chapter 3.

Adult Honduran Milksnakes typically do very well when fed appropriately-sized rodents once a week. Here again, you want to feed them a rodent that allows for a noticeable lump in their belly. If the single rodent isn't quite large enough to see a visible lump, offer it two prey items per feeding to make up the size difference.

During the breeding season, males can typically go off feed because of their natural instincts to stay trim and

© Rusty Green

actively seek female mates. Feeding them well coming out of winter brumation for a while is a good idea since you can anticipate that they will likely stop feeding later on. If you have already introduced the male to a female in hopes of them breeding, it can often make them stop feeding instantly knowing there are ovulating females in the immediate vicinity.

It is not recommended at all to house or feed more than one adult snake in a single enclosure. The genus *Lampropeltis* are known for eating other reptiles, including their own kind. Honduran Milksnakes are not as noted for cannibalism like the common kingsnakes are (*L.getula*), but it is always a possibility nonetheless. Some people do keep more than one snake together, but there can also be some serious consequences to this.

Things can often seem to go smoothly, even for a very long time until one fateful day when one of the occupants decides that there is another feeding opportunity living in the very same enclosure. There is simply no way to know when a catastrophe involving cannibalism can become a reality. Preventing this from happening in the first place is what you want to do, not find out for yourself after it does. There have been multiple reports of these unfortunate stories over the years.

Chapter 2
Purchasing a Honduran Milksnake

Today there are many options for purchasing Honduran Milksnakes. A traditional method would be a local pet shop to see what they have available. Even though it is quite possible to get healthy snakes from pet stores, it is recommended to seek out the breeders themselves if at all possible. This is because breeders usually offer detailed background information, the

TRICOLOR © Douglas Mong

EXTREME HYPO © Douglas Mong

GHOST © Rusty Green

TANGERINE © Douglas Mong

ANERYTHRISTIC © Douglas Mong

© Rusty Green

ability to personally inspect and choose your animal and in most cases offer lower prices.

Reptile shows are a great way to find a desired specimen for your collection. It also gives you the ability to meet local breeders and suppliers. In more recent years, another convenient way of purchasing a snake is through reputable

National Reptile Breeder's Expo in Daytona, Fl.

Outstanding Extreme Hypo hatchling.

Children viewing snakes displayed at a reptile show.

breeder websites, or online classified ads. There are also many reptile forums with "milksnake" sections in them to locate breeders that are much more knowledgeable than others. You can often get a "feel" for the sources that seem to be better in general, compared to going to someone "sight unseen" to purchase a snake. The information posted and talked about regarding other breeders can also be extremely useful when considering a snake purchase.

It is important to think of as many pertinent questions before purchasing your next addition. Depending on how you purchased your snake, contacting the seller may not be as easy after the sale.

These are all things that are very important to find out and to know. Not only to get a good general idea of the new snake you are buying, but for your personal records. This will help out immensely with future breeding projects, as well as the sale of any future offspring. There is plenty of extremely crucial information that gets forgotten or lost completely from not documenting and keeping good records.

The very first thing you should do if you are able to actually hold and look over a snake you are thinking about purchasing is to closely inspect it over for several things. Let it crawl in and out of your hands and fingers, and look and feel for overall good muscle tone and movement. Check the eyes closely and make sure they are nice and clear, and that there are no wrinkles or stuck eye caps from any previous shed(s). Look for any potential lumps, bumps or kinks along the entire body and closely inspect it for mites. Mites look like tiny dots of pepper on the snake's body and under the scales. A trick to easily inspect for mites is to let the snake crawl through a white tissue, or paper towel as you are holding it. Inspect this for any small black dots that may be present.

Take note of the snake's weight, and that it doesn't seem excessively thin from not eating from an underlying health issue. Make sure the snake's tongue is flicking in and out often as it moves through your hands. This is how a typical healthy snake behaves. Also closely inspect around the mouth to see that it is fully-closed and not gaping, crusty or bubbling with any mucus present.

The nostrils should also be nice and clean and free of any bubbles, crust or mucus discharge. The vent (cloaca) should also appear flush with the rest of the underside, and have no visible crusty substance around it. These things are usually never an issue with new hatchlings, but with older snakes that have possibly been subjected to poor maintenance and husbandry prior to you owning them. If you are having a snake (or snakes) shipped to your home or business, this obviously won't be something you can do until after arrival.

If you are receiving a shipment of snakes, the very SECOND you receive the box you should very closely inspect all contents for mites. This needs to be done in an area away from your other snakes. This is to ensure that there are no mites that will crawl out and get into the rest of your collection. At this time, you can follow the steps previously stated on inspection of the animal itself. Thoroughly inspect and wash your hands well after doing this. If any problems are seen, contact the seller immediately upon arrival.

A quarantine period of at least 60 to 90 days is highly recommended for any new acquisitions. This prevents any cross-contamination getting transferred anywhere else in the process.

Another very important reason for quarantining any new arrival, is so you can make sure the snake is feeding properly, defecating normally, and seems to be in very good overall health. When all seems well after the quarantine period, and none of the previously mentioned points are an issue, you can then setup the snake's enclosure permanently with any others.

IMPORTANT QUESTIONS to ASK

- When did the snake hatch?
- Has it fed? And what exactly did it eat?
- How often has it fed?
- What do the two parents look like that produced it?
- What are the parent's individual genetics, such as being recessive gene carriers for any traits (heterozygous, aka "het")?
- What, or who's particular bloodline did they originate from?
- Will they stand behind their snakes and offer help if something should arise later on?
- Are there any special feeding details or quirks that I need to know?

Handling Your Recent Purchase

How Honduran Milksnakes are handled is extremely important to keep in mind and especially with regards to young milksnakes. The initial experiences a tiny hatchling has with its keeper can make a big difference in how it perceives you now, and even later on. Remember though, don't be the slightest bit surprised or discouraged if your tiny hatchling sees you as something to avoid at all costs for a good while. This is simply how they stay alive in the wild, and is very typical of them at this early stage.

Most juvenile snakes are naturally very nervous and "head-shy" to begin with, and they will gradually outgrow this instinct. Baby milksnakes, and all others for that matter, basically see us as nothing less than giant "monsters" that want to do them bodily harm, or worse, eat them! This is quite natural, and is simply how they are "hard-wired" to survive. If they were far more casual about large animals moving about around them, they would most definitely fall prey to more predators too.

Over the decades of owning and working with these snakes, it is generally best to not handle hatchlings too much except for their basic maintenance. This would be things like feeding, cleaning and filling the bowl with fresh water. It is not necessary to take them out when doing some of these routine tasks. Just take the water bowl out, clean it, and add fresh water without disturbing the snake whenever possible.

The same thing applies to periodic spot-cleaning of feces until it is changed-out entirely. The snakes will usually stay hidden in their secure hides that are provided just as they naturally would. When done carefully without knocking their enclosures around, it allows them to stay hidden just as they were before.

When it is necessary to hold a hatchling, they can often be extremely flighty, and thrash violently from side to side in an attempt to escape the grasp of the big "monster", you! While they are squirming and thrashing about, they will often bite and musk, purging every bit of body content they possibly can in an effort to distract you and escape. Snakes have scent glands located just behind the cloaca. These scent glands secrete a liquid with a very distinct foul odor when they musk. This is a very typical defense mechanism snakes can do to make a threatening predator leave them alone, or even make them completely let go if attacked. Generally, it is best to simply allow them to be themselves at this stage of their lives. They will eventually outgrow this nervous behavior, and begin to settle down over time.

One way to handle them when necessary is to slowly and deliberately reach down and gently grasp the hatchling at approximately mid-body. Doing so toward the neck will instantly make the snake feel threatened, and make it jerk back immediately in a frightened manner. By the same token, grasping the snake toward the tail will only make it want to instinctively snatch its tail back and bolt-

Mega Hypomelanistic

Typical hatchling behavior while being restrained.

off. Grasp them just forward of mid-body, this allows them to move forward which they will typically do. By the time you gently pinch with your fingers enough to have a hold of it; you can then lift it up.

Next, gently lower the snake into your other free-hand and restrain them just enough to still allow them to continue to crawl through your fingers. Make sure you always have control, and don't let go until the snake crawls into your other hand to continue the process. This makes them feel much less restrained and in turn less fearful and defensive. This will allow them to gradually become accustomed to your non-threatening movements and scent.

As your snake crawls from hand to hand in an escalator motion, try not to let them view your free hand in their peripheral vision coming towards them. When this happens, it is viewed as a very threatening gesture. Slow, gentle motions are best. Let the young snake contact your hand first, as any harsh movements may spook the snake. Gradually the hatchling will become accustomed to these handling procedures and learn that you are not trying to harm them.

A small homemade hook made out of wire that has been smoothed and rounded at the end generally works very well for handling hatchlings. It stresses them far less than having your giant "monster hand" coming down upon them and grabbing them. Just make sure this is done on the floor or a large table, and that you are ready to grasp them quickly if they should bolt off the hook. You want to prevent them from falling and hurting themselves in the process, or disappearing into something completely if they should manage to get away.

After your snake has eaten, it is recommended that you do not handle them until the second or third day. The snake could regurgitate its meal if handled too soon. In the wild, snakes will use this as a defensive behavior. The expulsion of the partially digested meal is an attempt to distract the predator, so it can go on to live another day. Keep in mind that a captive snake if kept at optimum temperatures will defecate around this same time. Be prepared for this to happen if it hasn't done so prior to being handled.

After about ten months to a year, most start becoming much more manageable than they were as hatchlings. The first thing they will typically stop doing is the fearful defensive biting. The next thing to gradually subside is the musking and defecating. All it takes is some patience and to allow them to be what nature intended them to be, which are great instinctual survivors. By the time these snakes are sub-adults and adults, they have become far more used to being handled and much more acclimated to captivity and the scent of their owners. Most will be very accepting of handling, especially once they have been lifted out of their enclosures for just a few moments, and quickly adjust to being out. Some can remain a bit more nervous than others. It really depends on the individual snakes themselves, the inherent bloodline they came from and how they perceive their immediate surroundings. Like almost any other animal, snakes too are individuals and have their own little personalities.

Chapter 3
Seasonal Changes & Breeding

© Rusty Green

© Douglas Mong

Honduran Milksnakes are indigenous to Honduras, Nicaragua and just into the extreme northern edge of Costa Rica. Here, the fall and winter months are very mild compared to other colder parts of the world. With that said, they generally wouldn't necessarily need to be brumated at the colder temperatures and duration that many other types of milksnakes are kept at during this process.

Pictures depicting typical breeding behaviors

If you think about it, how often do temperatures ever get into the mid 50s and low 60s in Honduras or Nicaragua, especially in the lowlands where these snakes inhabit? Still though, they do need to sense a seasonal change with cooler temperatures and a shorter photoperiod. As the days become shorter and cooler with the onset of the fall season, your snakes will instinctively slow down their feeding, or possibly even stop altogether. This typically happens around October through December.

Brumation

Brumation is a term intended to loosely describe "hibernation" in reptiles and other cold-blooded animals, such as amphibians. The term "hibernation", what many mammals do is sometimes mistakenly applied by the general public for the proper term "brumation". The point of having two terms is that hibernation is a more complex process involving some regulation of body temperature, whereas brumation is a general slowing of all metabolic processes.

Prior to your snakes being prepared for the brumation process, it is extremely important that they have not been fed any meals for a period of approximately two weeks or more. This helps to ensure that their digestive tract is thoroughly emptied of all food and fecal matter. If this was not done and the snakes were placed in brumation, they would be at risk of the material rotting in their digestive tract, causing internal bacterial infection, and possibly death.

After preparing your snake for the brumation process, you can start lowering their temperatures by turning off all heat.

Make sure the daytime temperatures are still in the mid 70s. This should last for a few days before placing the snakes in the room they are to stay in. The room should be completely dark, and temperatures kept between 55 F – 65F. During this time, the snakes' metabolism will be slowed considerably, but they will still carry out periodic bodily functions. This includes defecating and drinking water, as well as orienting themselves in different positions. It is important to make sure their substrate is kept dry, and they have access to clean water at all times. Spot clean any feces or urates, and note any visible shedding or skin problems. It is important to not let the temperatures fluctuate too much, as it could cause the snakes to develop upper respiratory problems. These can be quite serious and many snakes have perished because of this.

With the males, these cooler temperatures will naturally stimulate their sperm production, known as spermatogenesis. With females, these same seasonal conditions will allow their bodies to adjust and later prepare for the development of egg follicles.

The brumation process usually lasts 90 days, but there are many breeders that have been successful with shorter periods too. Even though Honduran Milksnakes don't need to be cooled down into the low 50s, many breeders still choose to cool them just as they would other milksnakes and colubrids in their collection. This can benefit the keeper/breeder in two ways. The snakes will cycle and breed successfully, as well as give the breeder a break with feeding and maintenance during these cooler months.

The above is a typical brumation process, but depending on where you may live in the country or world, the seasonal changes that govern your snake's yearly activity can be noticed at different times. These can vary considerably from one year to the next. This will depend on your particular areas weather pattern on any given year.

Spring Warm Up and Resuming Feeding

In the early spring, bring your snakes out of brumation by slowly warming them back up a few degrees each day over a week to ten days. Also, allow the photoperiod either artificially or naturally to become longer. Offer their first meals when the temperatures have resumed back to what they were prior to brumation.

After all that time in brumation, most snakes will be ready to feed with great enthusiasm. Some may be a bit more reluctant to feed, but will generally resume within a short period of time. It is a good idea to start off with smaller meals because their digestive systems were dormant for such a long time. After they have successfully fed and defecated a few times, you can start increasing the size of their prey. With females, it is especially important that they start gaining good body weight, as this will stimulate ovulation. It is just as crucial with males, as they will sometimes fast once the females have ovulated. After roughly 4 to 6 weeks, the female will undergo her first post-brumation shed. At this time, the females will begin to smell particularly attractive because of the natural pheromones produced underneath the shed skin.

Courtship and Breeding Behavior

A few days after the female sheds you can usually start checking for follicles. Quite often, if you let the female crawl through your hands, you can feel her unfertilized ova. As she crawls forward apply just a bit of pressure to the underside of her belly with your index finger or thumb. These unfertilized ova that can be felt along her body are sometimes referred to as "the string of pearls". This is the time you want to pair the male up with her to see how they respond to each other. Many times the female will not be quite ready to breed, and this is very typical. The male will usually follow her around the enclosure flicking his tongue rapidly and moving along on top of her in short jerking motions. If the female is ready to breed, she will often begin to do these same movements along with him.

If the female is not ready to breed however, she will definitely let the male know about it by pulling her tail away to thwart off the male's advances. In her attempts to shake-off and flee the male, you can often see them knocking around in the enclosure. If this continues for more than a couple hours, separate the two and try again in a few days. It is a good idea to keep reintroducing them periodically like this to make sure the right "window

STRING of PEARLS

Quite often if you let the female crawl through your hands, you can feel her unfertilized egg follicles (ova) by applying just a bit of pressure to the underside of her belly with your index finger or thumb as she crawls forward. These unfertilized ova that can be felt along her body are sometimes referred to as "the string of pearls" by seasoned breeder aficionados. This is the time you want to pair the chosen male up with her to see how they respond to each other.

The Guide to Honduran Milksnakes

of opportunity" is not missed. Sometimes it will be the same situation until after her next shed.

Don't be discouraged by this in the least, because this can often be typical. It can sometimes take two or even three sheds for the female to finally settle down and decide when she is ready to breed.

You can tell when things are going better when her movements become slower and more relaxed. At this point, she will begin lifting her tail slightly and open her cloaca. This is known as "cloacal gaping". The male will then align his with hers and insert one of his hemipenes.

Copulation can last anywhere from twenty minutes to a couple of hours. If you are there, and are able to witness the copulation, don't disturb them. Move very slowly so the snakes don't get startled and begin moving around noticing your presence. You certainly don't want the female to start dragging the male around by his hemipenis. Just come back periodically, and see how they are doing. If you are not sure they actually did copulate try to make a mental note of where their tails were the last time they were entwined and look for any evidence of sperm. This is always a great sign that they copulated.

Once copulation has occurred, you want to keep introducing the pair for at least another week or more. Some breeders prefer to leave them together for several days at a time. Keep this up until you notice that the female doesn't want anything more to do with the male. Hopefully, you'll see her midsection swell and become noticeably gravid. These successive copulations help to ensure that all the female's eggs are fertilized. After all, only one of the male's two sperm ducts is ever utilized in any single copulation.

Many people that have been breeding snakes for years are not even aware of this interesting fact. Every time a male breeds, 9 times out of 10 he will use the opposite side hemipenis that he last used. There is one of these sex organs located on each side of the snake, situated inside the base of the tail just past the vent. The reason for nature doing this is two-fold. One, it allows a male to breed the female again should they stay close together. This also allows the male to have a new supply of sperm for the next mating. Or two, if the male should come across another female shortly after breeding the first, he has another fresh supply.

A Collective History of Honduran Milksnakes for the Hobbyist

Egg-Laying and Incubation

Egg-laying puts many stresses on the female snake. In turn, the female can utilize more calories at this time. She will deplete most of her resources with the expense of producing the eggs. Usually, feeding the female at closer intervals will help with replacing these. If you plan on double-clutching your females, now is the time to make sure she has plenty of food. She will not have more than roughly 6 weeks to recuperate before laying eggs again.

Keep up the good feeding schedule for as long as possible until you notice her getting more reluctant about accepting food. As she swells more and more, she will typically be less enthusiastic

about feeding. Try offering her rodents about a third of the size of what she was previously eating. Many times they will accept these much smaller offerings. It only makes good sense that now there isn't nearly as much room inside her for processing food. Keep feeding her one or two of these smaller prey items every few days if she will accept them. By the time she refuses all prey, you will know egg-laying is not far away.

From the time of breeding to actual egg-laying, it will typically take anywhere from between 30 to 45 days. Prior to actually depositing the eggs, she will have what is known as a "pre-lay" shed. This can take place anywhere from about 5 to 12 days before the eggs are deposited.

In anticipation of her laying the eggs, it is extremely important that you set up a nesting box for her to get familiar with well before she actually lays eggs. By placing a nesting box in beforehand, this will alleviate the stress of finding a suitable nesting site. When females can't locate a proper place to lay their eggs, they can sometimes become "egg-bound". This is also commonly referred to as "egg retention", and medically known as dystocia.

The lay box can be a plastic shoe box

© Rusty Green

filled with moistened sphagnum moss, peat moss or vermiculite. There needs to be an entrance hole cut either in the side, or in the plastic lid for her to go in and out of. This hole should be at least one and one-half times her diameter to allow her easy access in and out. Using a plastic container will help contain the moisture and humidity, as well as make her feel better hidden and secure.

Depending on how large your female is, you can also make one entire side of her enclosure a suitable nesting site. All this involves is placing enough nesting medium until it seems adequate for her to crawl into and be well-hidden and secure. Placing a heavy lid or ceramic serving dish on top of the nesting medium will give her the needed security. Another method would be to use a piece of plexi-glass over the nesting medium and a piece of plywood on top of that. This will allow you to carefully lift the plywood and check on her periodically so she won't be disturbed or startled while laying her eggs.

As mentioned previously, have this all done prior to her pre-lay shed just in case she is an exception and lays them a bit earlier than expected.

During the course of this, you will

Several days after being laid, you can clearly see the developing embryo and veins in this egg being candled.

© Rusty Green

Notice the yellow coloration on these infertile eggs.

© Douglas Mong

(below) Clutch of good eggs. Notice the "X" on the loose egg depicting the top.

© Douglas Mong

see her periodically roaming in and out of the box determining where she will ultimately settle down to lay her eggs. If housed in an aquarium or something similar, you can drape a towel over the top for her enclosure to feel more secure. Roughly seven to ten days after her pre-lay shed, she will become less active. You will notice her spending more time in here nesting site. When this happens, you can expect egg deposition in a day or so.

In the prior days to egg deposition, the female may sometimes lay one or several infertile eggs outside the lay box. This can be typical, so don't be alarmed and let the female continue on. Many times these eggs will be infertile, but not always. If they seem to be good viable eggs, carefully collect them and place them in the incubating medium you have prepared.

If you are using a clear or opaque plastic container for her nesting box, you can gently lift it up and look in from underneath without disturbing her to see how she is doing. It will typically take several hours to 24 hours to complete the egg laying process. As your excitement grows, it is important to be patient and not to disturb the female. Once she is done depositing her eggs, you can remove them from her. Make sure that you visually inspect and feel down the female's body to be certain that there are no eggs still inside her. Give her 24 hours to recuperate and regain some energy before offering food. Once again, starting with somewhat smaller meals and increasing the size afterwards.

As you remove the eggs you can inspect them for viability. Eggs are usually laid in a single clump and stuck together. There can be single eggs here and there that are not stuck to the rest of the clutch. If you find obvious infertile eggs, you can often carefully separate them from the rest at this time. Usually the very noticeable infertile eggs don't have the "gluing" ability of good eggs. In order to separate them, you must slowly pull them away from the others in a very slow and gentle prying motion. Be extremely careful not to damage the surrounding good eggs. Depending on the amount of time between them being laid, their individual shell condition and when you remove them from the female, it can sometimes be impossible to do. If you notice them starting to tear when you attempt this, it is best just to leave them as a whole entire clutch.

As you set your eggs up in their incubating medium, make sure you do not rotate them in any manner. Once again, this is all dependent on the amount of time between them being laid and when you remove them from the female. Soon after the egg is laid the embryo will attach itself to the inner egg wall membrane towards the top. There is a little pocket of air within the egg that the embryo needs to expel carbon dioxide. It is then released through the leathery shell surface. If you rotate the egg too long after being laid, you can risk suffocating the embryo with the albumin that is inside. This is why it is a good idea to mark the upright tops of loose single eggs in the orientation they were first laid with a small pen mark or water-based marker. This lets you know just how they were situated in case any get accidentally turned during the course of checking and maintaining the incubating medium. Eggs that inadvertently get turned can also hatch, but why take the chance when you can simply mark them.

Fertile/Infertile eggs

Just as it can sometimes happen in nature, herpetoculturists will also experience some infertile eggs from time to time. Sometimes entire clutches will be laid that are simply not fertile, and this can be caused by any number of things.

- male was too young and did not produce viable sperm.
- window of opportunity was missed as the ova was released into the oviduct
- female couldn't develop proper calcification around the eggs.
- male was kept too warm, thus killing his viable sperm.

For the average hobbyist, or even the experienced breeder, these are not always things that can easily be concluded. Even from one year to the next and with

the very same pairing things can still go wrong. One can only make fairly educated guesses as to any of the reasons why this can happen.

Good viable eggs are typically a white or slightly off-white coloration with a firm "leathery" porous texture. Infertile eggs are usually obvious, but there can be definite exceptions. They can be darkish yellow to beige, or a soft rubbery texture and often smaller than the rest.

After several days to a week have past, you can "candle" the eggs to get a good idea of their fertility. All this takes is a small penlight with a LED bulb that doesn't give off any heat held against them for a few seconds. Fertile eggs will illuminate with a pinkish coloration and have small veins along the inner wall of the egg. Infertile eggs will glow a yellowish coloration with no visible veins.

Nevertheless, if there is ANY question at all about the viability of any eggs, there is no good reason to discard them until you know for certain they are obviously spoiled. You can continue to incubate them along with the others, or if you have a doubt of the viability, you can set them up in a different container. Again, make sure when you move the eggs not to rotate

TYPES
of
INCUBATION MEDIUMS

- **Hatch Rite®**
- **Vermiculite**
- **Perlite**
- **Sphagnum Moss**
- **Peat Moss**
- **Coconut Peat**

them. If mold is forming on any eggs in the clutch, you can lightly dust them with an anti-fungal foot powder. This can be found at your local drugstore or pharmacy section of any department store.

Incubation

The incubation of Honduran eggs is pretty basic and straightforward. There are a few basic requirements they need to properly incubate and hatch.

1) incubating medium
2) ventilation
3) humidity
4) temperature

First, you need a container sufficient enough for the eggs, incubating medium and proper air exchange. Drill or melt a few 1/8th inch holes about three inches apart in the containers top. The holes should not be too numerous or large that they dry out the incubating medium. The incubating medium can consist of various different materials.

Most herpetoculturists still use the time-proven materials, vermiculite or perlite as an incubating medium. These can be purchased at any nursery or home improvement center. If straight vermiculite or perlite is used, it is better to use the courser granule type. However, the more commonly found smaller granule type can have very successful hatching results just the same. When purchasing either one, make sure there are no additives, such as fertilizers. The coarser granules will allow better air circulation to discourage any mold or mildew growth. Perlite seems to be more forgiving when it comes to having a bit too much moisture content when compared to the vermiculite.

To get the proper ratio of water to vermiculite, perlite or a combination of the two, use a 1:1 ratio by weight (not volume). Add the water little by little as you continue mixing until it is all combined thoroughly. Next, take a tiny handful and squeeze it together in your fist. It should just clump together well, and not want to crumble apart. If it crumbles, just add more water very slowly as you mix it until it stays together. If you squeeze it and it drips any water, you have too much water and will then need to add more medium and re-mix thoroughly. Once you have the correct consistency, fill the container with 1 ½ to 2 inches of this mixture.

Now it is time to place the eggs in the incubating container with the medium you've mixed. Gently make a dimpled "cradle" into the surface of the substrate with your knuckle. Place the individual eggs in each dimple with a couple of gentle back and forth motions. You want at least half the egg to be exposed above the incubating mediums surface. If the eggs are stuck together in a cluster, just leave them that way and situate the entire pile into the medium just as you did with the individual eggs. The pile of eggs will basically act like a sponge, and the middle and upper eggs in the clutch will absorb moisture from each neighboring egg. If you notice that the upper eggs are starting to dimple, moisten some sphagnum moss, fluff it up and drape it over the eggs. This will allow them to receive the necessary moisture and resume their normal appearance. It is very important to keep periodic tabs on them during the time they are incubating. Remember, without enough moisture, the eggs will dry up and die. With too much, they will swell up and suffocate the embryo, and possibly rupture. Either way the embryos will perish.

Incubating Temperatures

Snake eggs can often hatch successfully with a fairly wide range of temperatures. It is always best to target a temperature that is slightly cooler if something should go wrong during the process, such as temperature fluctuations or spikes. The slightly lower temperature allows for a small "buffer zone" of insurance. A good target temperature would be 79 to 81 degrees Fahrenheit. With these temperatures, they will hatch anywhere from about 73 to 80 days or so. Additionally, many breeders have found that these temperatures, or slightly cooler allow the embryo to more fully absorb the yolk, and can hatch a bit more robust in size.

Some herpetoculturists will allow a slight nighttime drop in temperature by just a few degrees. It is thought that this might give the embryos some time to relax in between the developing stages of incubation. Generally in nature, the females choose nesting sites that have good constant optimal temperatures. One has to wonder if there isn't a slight drop in many of their nests at nighttime in nature. This would all depend on precisely where the sites were, what they were made of, facing what direction, and many other factors. There could very well be something to this, and it's something that is hard to say with absolute certainty. To conclude as hard fact, it would involve some very accurately controlled tests with many animals over the course of years. In any case though, it does seem very plausible.

From time to time you may encounter fertile eggs that just don't make it full-term. Your conditions could be optimal, and still have some go bad, while others

A Collective History of Honduran Milksnakes for the Hobbyist

hatch just fine. The failure for these eggs to hatch can be caused by various things during their incubation. Other causes can also be due to lethal genes within the DNA of the parents, or there could be severe deformities within the embryo for any number of unknown reasons. Most breeders that have been doing this for any length of time have all experienced this sort of thing at one time or another. Certain things will always remain out of the keeper's control. The important thing is to keep temperature, humidity and ventilation at optimum levels to keep these unwanted possibilities to an absolute minimum.

After around 65 days or more of incubation depending on all the factors, the eggs may start to dimple a little bit, but not always. This is a good sign that the baby snakes will be using their egg tooth to slit the egg to emerge fairly soon. Once the eggs are slit (known as pipping), it can often happen in multiple places along the egg as the neonate pushes its snout back and forth to penetrate the leathery shell. Then you will see the hatchling's tiny snout or entire head emerge from the egg and begin taking its first breaths of life. The baby snakes will stay tucked inside of the egg with only their heads exposed breathing from 24 to 48 hours before fully emerging. During this time, the

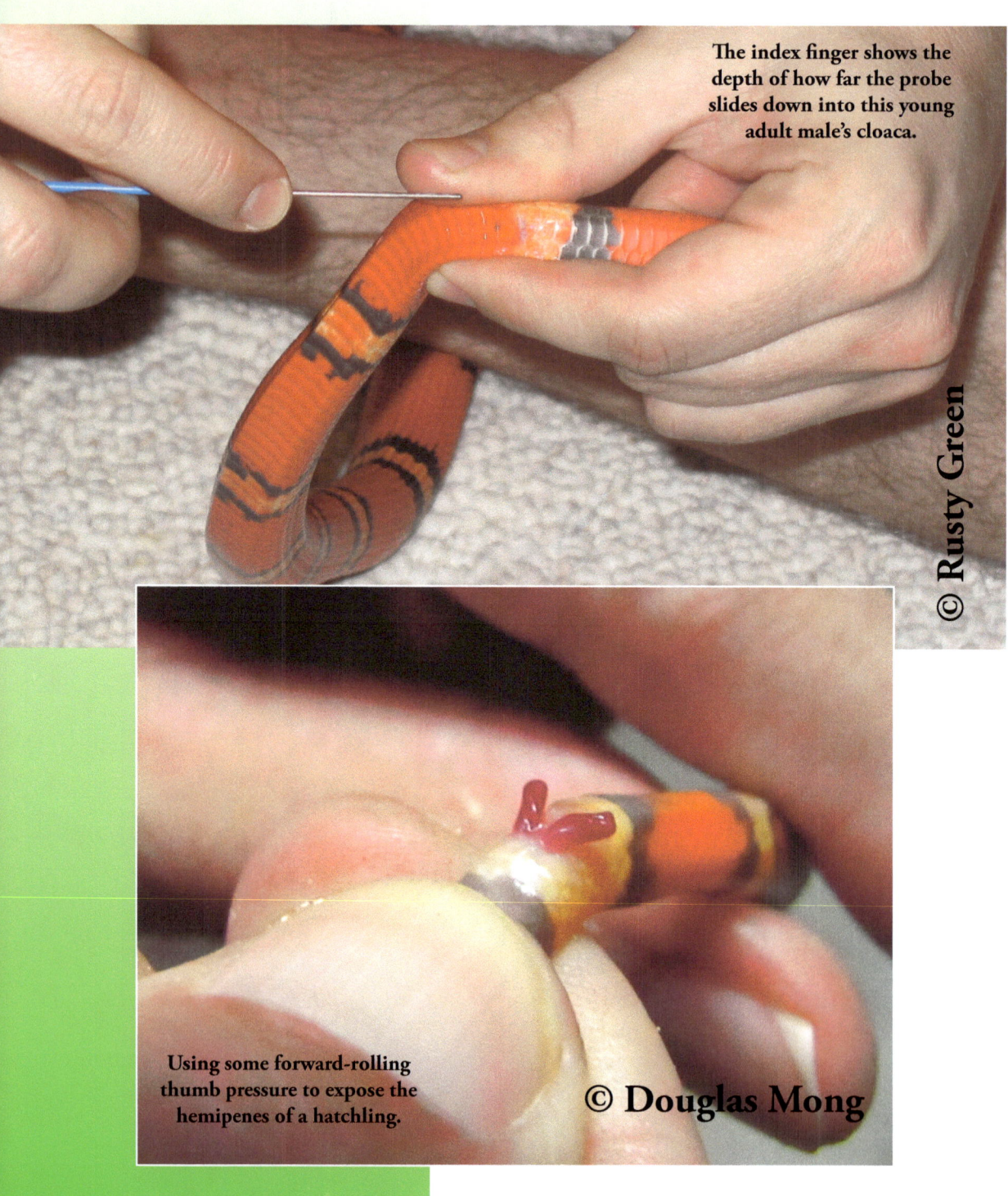

The index finger shows the depth of how far the probe slides down into this young adult male's cloaca.

© Rusty Green

Using some forward-rolling thumb pressure to expose the hemipenes of a hatchling.

© Douglas Mong

hatchling is absorbing the rest of the yolk sac. Do not ever forcefully remove the baby snake from the egg, as this can easily cause the demise of the neonate.

Sometimes a hatchling will emerge with the yolk sac still attached to the body. It is a good idea to remove this snake from the rest of the clutch. Place the neonate in a small secure container with moist paper towels until it fully absorbs its yolk sac and the umbilical cord has dried up and is completely disconnected from the body.

The neonates will shed 7-10 days after emerging from the egg. At this time you can separate the neonates from the others and set them up in their new housing arrangements.

Sexing Hatchlings

After the hatchlings have shed for the first time you can then sex them. Sexing hatchlings is pretty easy to do, as long as you understand how to do it properly. If this isn't done correctly you can severely injure the hatchling, or even cause it to die. Many inexperienced people have killed their tiny hatchlings by incorrectly sexing them.

Most herpetoculturists prefer to do what is known as "popping" the hatchlings. When they are small, they have very little strength and muscle control developed in their tails to resist this method. Hold the hatchling's tail portion ventral side up, and starting about a half-inch or so past the vent. Next, apply sufficient pressure and roll the tip of your thumb forward towards the vent at the same time. When doing this correctly, if it is a male hatchling, this forward-rolling pressure will force out and expose their hemipenes, one popping out from each side. With females, nothing will protrude or be exposed on either side. The only exception is the possibility of seeing just two tiny darkish dots at the tips of two small bulges, one on each side of the vent opening. These are the female's scent glands.

Probing is another way of sexing hatchlings, and this technique works best for juveniles to adults. This involves a thin, smooth round-tipped stainless steel rod that is lubricated with vegetable oil, mineral oil, petroleum or water-based lubricants. Gently slide the instrument into one side of the cloacal opening. As you VERY gently slide it in towards the tail tip, use a slight twisting motion as you go. This will help it along and give you a much better "feel" for any slight resistance. If the probe goes down 4 or more individual subcaudal scales, it's a male. If it gently bottoms-out at 4 or less subcaudal scales, it's a female. Either method MUST be done very carefully to prevent serious injury to the snake! If you have never done this before, it is highly recommended that you seek someone out that has personal experience with doing these procedures. Reptile shows, local pet stores and veterinarians that deal with reptiles can often have someone there that can do this for you.

Chapter 4
Genetics

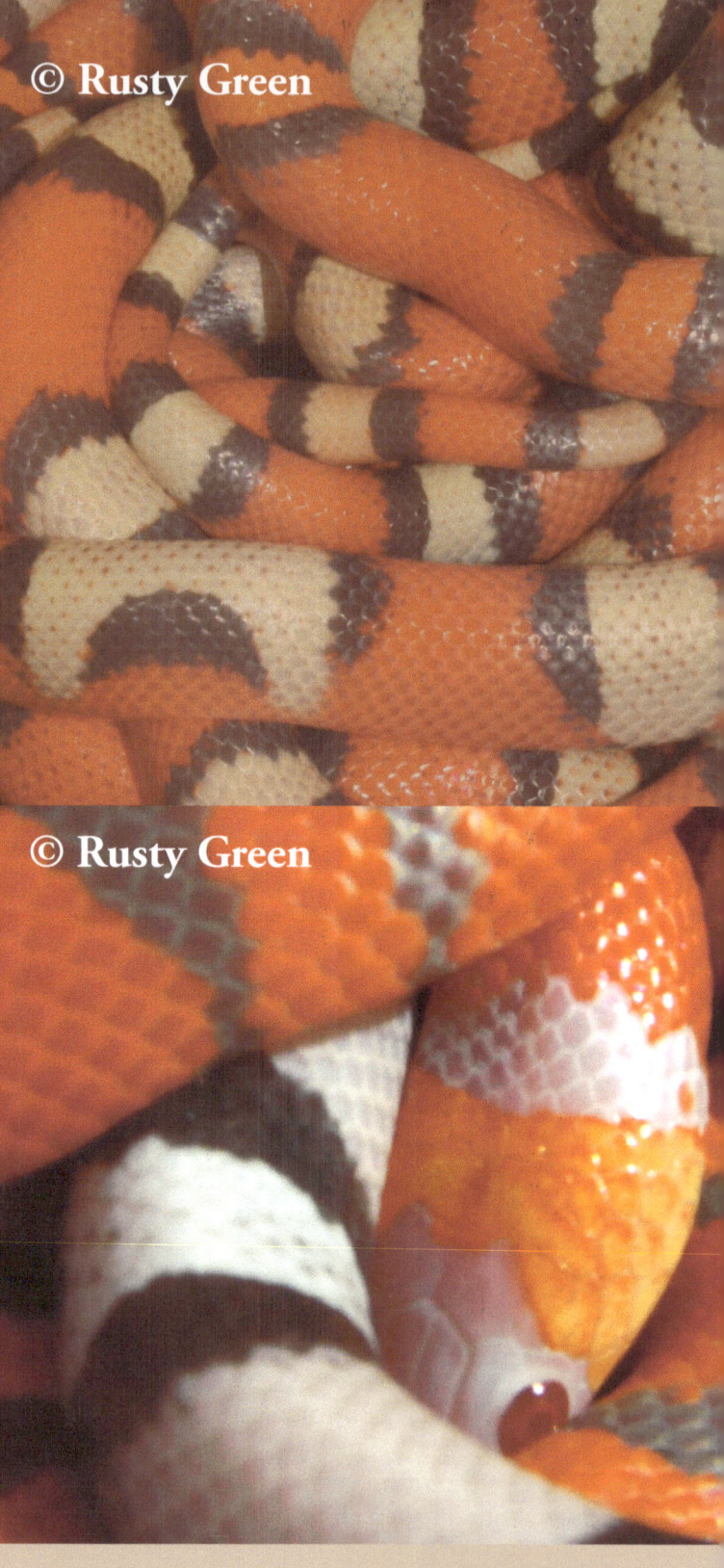

© Rusty Green

© Rusty Green

(top) Tricolor and tangerine hypomelanistics. (bottom) Hypomelanistic, ghost and amelanistic .(opposite page) Amelanistic, extreme hypomelanistic and ghost.

The Guide to Honduran Milksnakes

© Don Shores

Snake genetics can be a very exciting and rewarding endeavor. Understanding how it works will allow you to selectively pair different mutations and combinations together to produce very specific outcomes you might desire. With this knowledge, you can also prove or disprove hidden genetic traits in snakes you may own that have unknown genetic backgrounds. Understanding the genetic possibilities of what can be produced in a given clutch of eggs can also save you years of wasted time. Once these basic fundamentals are understood, the sky can be the limit. With all of the different mutations and combinations available today, who knows; you could even produce a morph that has never yet been seen before!. The following information will help you get a very good understanding of how the different recessive genes in Honduran Milksnakes are inherited.

A Collective History of Honduran Milksnakes for the Hobbyist

GENETIC PRINCIPLES

Visual traits occur when two genes (one from each parent) pair up together on the chromosome.

"Alternate forms of the same gene are called alleles" (*Medical Genetics: Principles & Practice, by Nora & Fraser*)

All the popular Honduran morphs are recessive gene mutations.

(such a mutation is called recessive because if paired with another, "dominant" gene, the recessive gene recedes into the background because it is overpowered by the dominant gene and the dominant gene determines the color and/or pattern of the animal.

An animal with two different mutant genes or alleles, one recessive and one "normal" or dominant, looks "normal" and is called heterozygous or het ("hetero" = "different") for that recessive mutation.

An animal with two genes for the same trait then shows the trait and is called homozygous ("homo" = "same") for that mutation.

An animal with two genes for the same recessive trait shows the recessive trait and is called "homozygous" for that mutation.

When parents breed, the father's sperm joins the mother's ovum, with each parent contributing one gene from each pair to each offspring.

A homozygous parent has two of the recessive genes, so it always passes on a recessive gene to every offspring it produces.

A heterozygous parent (with one recessive gene and one dominant or "normal" gene) will contribute a recessive gene to half its babies, and a "normal" gene to the other half.

Referenced from Terry Dunham's "Albino Tricolors" website

BREEDING EXPECTATIONS

Remember, these generalizations apply to large samples. In small numbers, such as the total number of eggs a female might produce in a clutch, or even in a lifetime the results can vary greatly, just as the odds of tossing heads or tails with a coin are always 50-50 but you will not always throw two heads in four tosses, or ten in twenty, etc…

SINGLE-MUTATION BREEDING EXPECTATIONS

homozygous x homozygous (*eg. albino x albino*)

= All homozygous (albinos, in this example)
Every baby is going to get a recessive (albino) gene from each parent, because that's all each parent has to contribute, so all the babies will end up with TWO albino genes, making all of them albinos (amelanistic homozygotes).

homozygous x heterozygous (*eg. hypo x het/hypo*)

= 1/2 homozygous (hypos, in this example)
= 1/2 heterozygous (het/hypos)

Every baby will get a recessive (hypo) gene from the homozygous (hypo) parent, because that's all that parent has to contribute, the het parent will contribute hypo genes half the time, and normal genes half the time, so half the babies will get two hypo genes and will be hypos, and the other half will get one hypo gene and one normal gene and will be hets.

heterozygous x heterozygous (*eg. het /anerythristic x het /anerythristic*)

= 1/4 homozygous (anerythristics, in this example)
= 1/2 heterozygous (het/anerythristics)
= 1/4 normal

The father, who has one anerythristic gene and one "normal" gene will give anerythristic genes to half the babies and normal genes to the other half, the mother will do likewise. Half the babies that got anerythristic genes from the father will get an anerythristic gene from the mother too, so they will have two anerythristic genes (one from each parent) and will BE anerythristics. They will make up 1/4 of the offspring (half of half). Half of the babies that got normal genes from the father will get normal genes from the mother too, so they will have two normal genes, and will be 100% normal in every aspect and will make up 1/4 of the total offspring. The other 2/4 (or one-half) of the babies get an anerythristic gene from one parent and a normal gene from the other, so they are hets. Remember, the hets and the normals look alike and combined, make up 3/4 of the production. But two out of three of those normal-looking babies are actually hets, so we call those normal-looking babies "possible hets" with 2/3 chance of being het, or "2/3 chance possible hets". They're either hets or they're not, but you won't know which are which, so we use terminology that correctly characterizes the likelihood of their being hets.

A Collective History of Honduran Milksnakes for the Hobbyist

DOUBLE-MUTATION BREEDING EXPECTATIONS

double-het x double-het (*eg. double-het for snow*)

Think of this pairing as TWO het x het pairings combined (one, of het/albino x het/albino, and the other, of het/anery x het/anery): Remember the het x het explanation above? The het/alb x het/alb portion of this breeding will produce 1/4 albinos, 2/4 het/albinos, and 1/4 normals. Remember, too, that the het/anery x het/anery pairing will produce babies, 1/4 of which are anerythristic (and 2/4 of which are het/anery, and 1/4 of which are normal). Consider a sample of 16 babies, which is necessary to illuminate the results here: FOUR of the babies will be albinos, as I've just explained, 1/4 of all the babies will be anerythristic, so ONE (one-fourth) of those four albino babies will be anerythristic as well. Anerythristic-albinos are snows, so 1/16 of the babies (1/4 of 1/4) will be snows. Continuing that logic and those calculations results in the full breakdown below:

= 1/16 Homozygous (snows)
= 2/16 albino het/anerythristic
= 1/16 albino
= 2/16 anerythristic het/albino
= 4/16 double-hets for albino and anerythristic
= 2/16 het/albino
= 1/16 anerythristic
= 2/16 het/anerythristic
= 1/16 normal

Notice that there will be 3/16 that are visibly albino: one is an albino with no anerythristic "blood" and two are albinos that are also het/anery. Since 2/3 of these albinos are het/anerythristic and 1/3 is not, I refer to these as "albino 2/3 chance het/anerythristics" elsewhere (2/3 will be het/anery but you can't tell which). Similarly, 2/3 of the animals that are visibly anerythristic are also het/albino, so the visible (homozygous) anerythristics would be called "anerythristics 2/3 chance het/albino". Nine of 16 would be normal-looking, and of those nine, four would be double-hets, two would be het/albino, two would be het/anerythristic and one would be perfectly normal.....those would then be termed "possible double hets".

double homozygous x double-het (*eg. snow x double-het for snow*)

This pairing shows how understanding genetics can make a big difference in your results:
= 1/4 double-hets
= 1/4 albino het/anerythristic
= 1/4 anerythristic het/albino
= 1/4 snows

You can see just how efficient it is by comparing it to the results of the double-het x double-het pairing described earlier. Out of 16 babies, that double-het pairing produces NINE different kinds of snakes genetically, with FOUR different appearances, and the genetic makeup of only ONE of those 16 (the snow) is known with certainty.

When a double-homozygous animal is substituted for one of the double-hets in the pairing, however, only FOUR different kinds of snakes genetically are produced, and ALL FOUR are distinguishable visually. Furthermore, the production of snows is quadrupled and the production of albinos and anerythristics is increased, and those animals have the added advantage of always being definite hets for the other mutation.

Instead of 15 snakes out of 16 whose genetic composition is uncertain, there are none. Still, the double-het x double-het pairings are necessary to GET the double-homozygous animals that produce such improved results, or the even more dramatic but possibly less interesting results, below.

double-homozygous x double-homozygous (*eg. snow x snow*)

= ALL snow babies

TRIPLE HET BREEDING EXPECTATIONS

This is one of the most fantastic genotypes imaginable. A single pair of triple-hets will produce albinos, anerythristics, hypos, ghosts, snows, and hybinos! We won't go into the precise percentages of these here, but think of these snakes as being three different kinds of double hets. So you'll get roughly one-sixteenth ghosts, one-sixteenth snows, one-sixteenth hybinos, three-sixteenth albinos, three-sixteenth anerythristics, three sixteenth hypos and the small remaining number of normal-looking babies which will be "possible" triple hets since you won't know which ones are genetic carriers and which ones are not of any of the three specific traits.

PUNNETT SQUARE CONCEPT

amel x heterozygous amel used in this example

The mother's genetic contribution on top, the father's on the left side. (See Figure 1) Then simply add each one from the top and side in the intersecting space as done below......

Now that it has been filled out, we have 2/4 = 50% albinos and 2/4 = 50% het albinos. Each egg has a 50% chance of being albino or het albino. All the normal-looking offspring from this pairing have one albino gene. This means that if you cross a visual recessive (homozygous) animal with any heterozygous animal, all the normal-looking offspring will be 100% het for that recessive trait. (See Figure 2)

You can do this with any recessive gene or combination(s). There are also many different genetic calculators that are online now to help you figure out all sorts of different traits and multi-morph breeding combinations. After these basic concepts are understood and you get more familiar with them, you will be able to visualize many of the simpler outcomes right in your head. Just keep in mind, for any offspring to be a visual homozygous animal; they MUST have one identical copy from each parent. The online calculators are extremely handy for figuring out the double and triple morphs of Hondurans, as well as even quadruple and beyond combinations that some of the other types of snakes in the hobby now have.

In a typical Punnett Square the capital "A" represents the dominant normal phenotype parent. The lowercase "a" represents the recessive genes of the other parent. In this example it is the father.

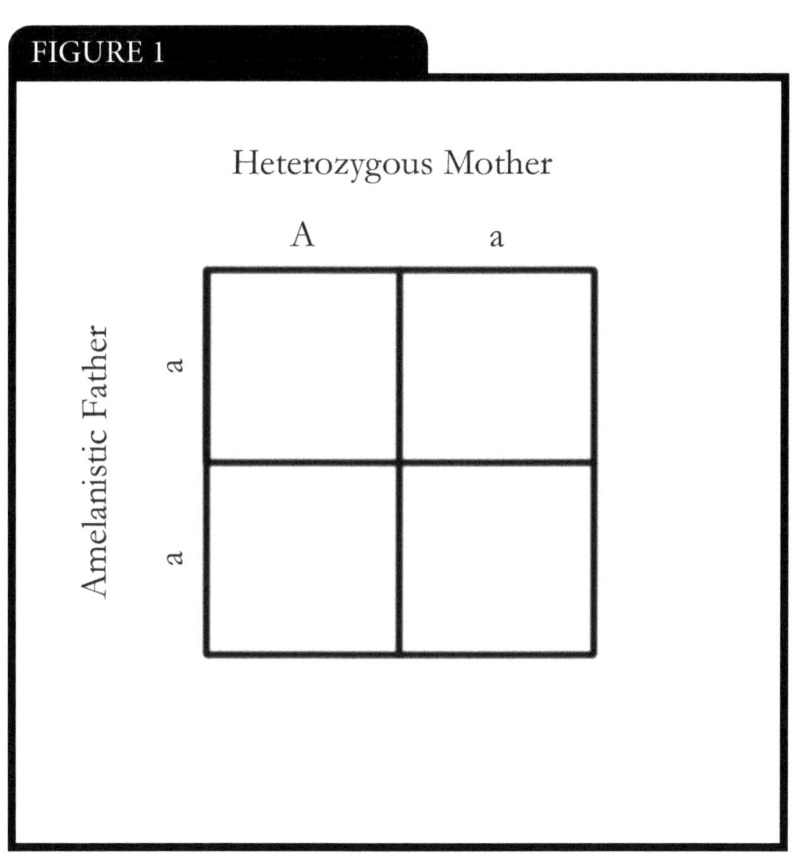

FIGURE 1

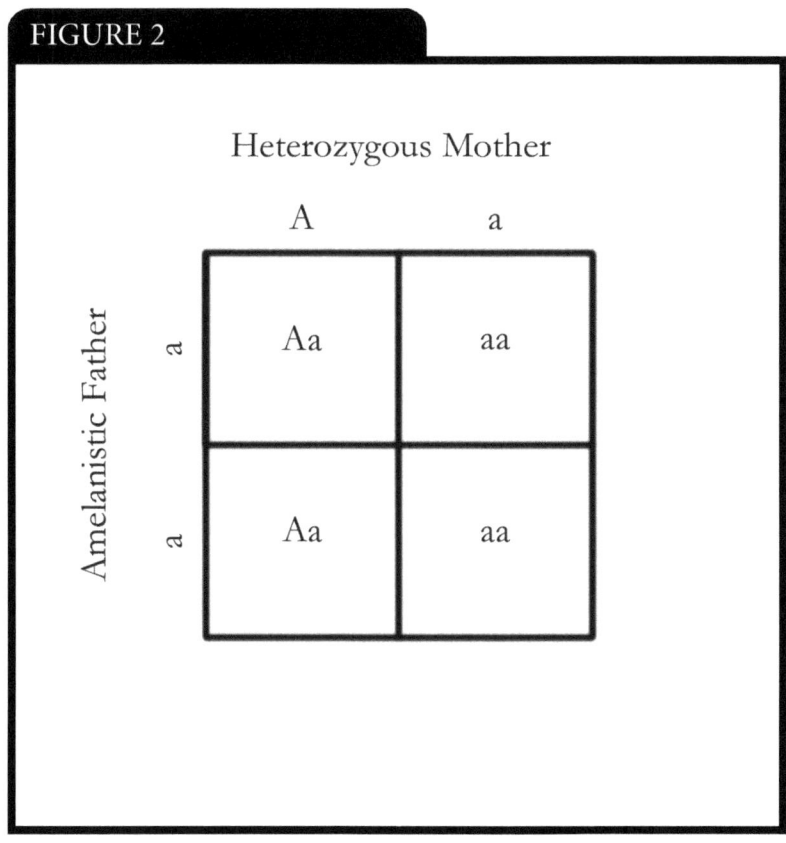

FIGURE 2

PIGMENTS AND PREFIXES

3 TYPES OF PIGMENTS

melanin (dark pigment; black, and varying shades of gray or brown)

erythrin (red pigmentation)

xanthin (yellow pigmentation)

Clean intermediate adult tricolor Honduran.

© Don Shores

Gorgeous example of a tricolor pin-banded hypo.

© Don Shores

PREFIXES

"**A**" or "**An**" before the word means the total absence of. (e.g. Amelanistic, Anerythristic and Axanthic)

"**Hypo**" means the reduction of. (e.g. Hypomelanistic, Hypoerythristic and Hypoxanthic)

"**Hyper**" means the exaggeration or overabundance of. (e.g. Hypermelanistic, Hypererythristic and Hyperxanthic)

The pigment cells (chromatophores) responsible for producing these pigments:

Melanin (melanophores)

Erythrin (erythrophores)

Xanthin (xanthophores)

There can often be a very complex dynamics going on between these last two types of pigment cells. Xanthophores produce both red and yellow pigments known as pteridines. These can vary in color from pure yellow to pure red, or any intermediate shade between these two colors. Xanthophores that possess a predominantly red coloration are referred to as erythrophores. Therefore, the distinction between these two types of chromatophores is not always clear. Varying shades of orange are a perfect example of this.

Chapter 5
Single Genetic Mutations

Anerythristic

The term "amelanistic" (amel) literally means the complete absence of dark pigment (melanin). This means in the pattern of the snake where it would normally be black, such as on the head and the two outer triad rings (ring sets of three) that go all the way down the snake's body, it will be white instead. These amelanistic snakes will also display red or pink eyes because there

Photographs by Douglas Mong

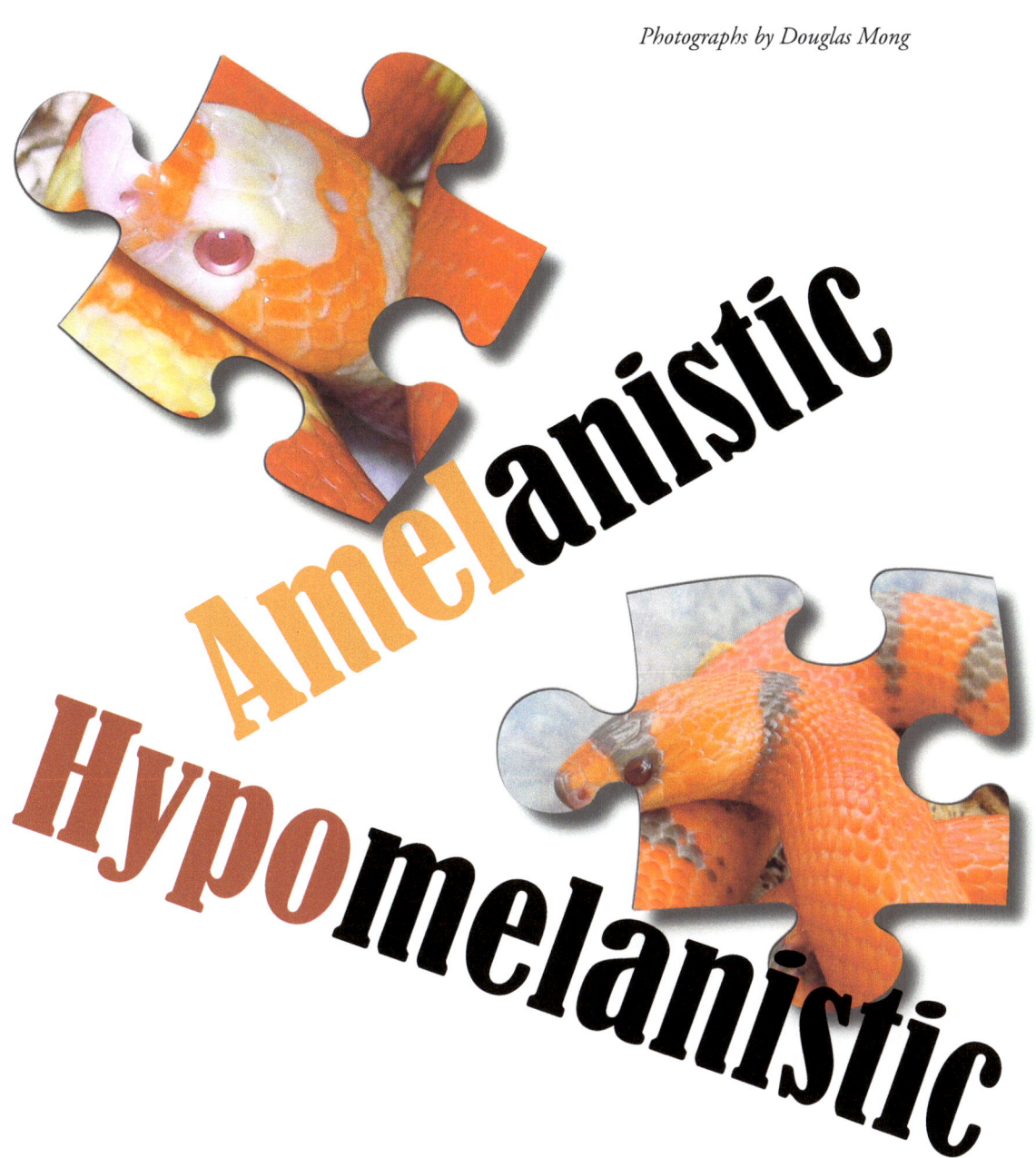

Amelanistic
Hypomelanistic

is no melanin deposited within the eye either. Additionally, since there is no dark pigment anywhere at all on the body, there is also no dark scale "tipping" that is typically seen on normally pigmented Honduran Milksnakes. This leaves the remaining colors very vivid and bright when compared to a normal wild type. Some individuals can also develop a yellowish or greenish tint to their white rings later on as they mature, and can sometimes be very pronounced. Some amelanistic individuals can also develop white or yellowish scale tipping as they mature due to the pattern not changing, but the color itself has within the scales. Instead of the normal dark tipping, it is light-colored because they are amelanistic and void of all dark pigment.

(Top) Louis W. Porras' original group of amelanistic Honduran Milksnakes and a heterozygous animal that he brought in to the US in 1995.

(Left) One of the first amelanistics Louis W. Porras hatched out from his breeding.

Amelanistic showing the yellow tipping.

A composite of Louis Porras' and Brian Barczyk's story told by Terry Dunham.

"The first known amelanistics were produced in a town near Liepzig in former East Germany back in 1989. Breeders Holger and Gabriele Hortenbach hatched this mutant amelanistic, and ironically there was little interest for these types of amelanistic morphs in Europe at the time. Some of the Hortenbach's friends even suggested that they kill it! Fortunately, they knew better than to do this and went on to produce many more.

Then in 1995, Louis Porras purchased several amels, bringing this morph to the United States and producing some that year and again in 1996 and 1997. Louis remembers "trembling with emotion" as he began unpacking them from the box. As he took the first out of its bag, he described it as "beautiful beyond words". Louis went on to produce amelanistics right away that same year and began selling them for $3,000 each in advance, along with his ambitious VHS marketing video.

It turns out Louis' amels were not the first to arrive in the U.S., because in 1994 Brian Barczyk (of BHB Enterprises) purchased two of what were called amelanistic "Atlantic Central American Milksnakes" (L.t.polyzona) babies and the trio of normal phenotypic snakes that produced them. These also came from Germany. When Louis' amelanistics hit the market, Brian investigated his own. He found out that they traced back to a dealer who got them from a couple who produced them using at least some animals they had also acquired from the Hortenbach's. The Hortenbach's were the very same people Louis bought his amels from. Brian and Louis both concluded and agreed that their amels were L.t.hondurensis. However, other knowledgeable people in the hobby thought they were in fact Atlantic Central American Milksnakes. After generations of the original amels being out-bred to many other "Hondurans" in the general hobby mainstream that were of unknown origins, they cannot be considered pure authentic L.t.hondurensis or L.t.polyzona."

(above) An interesting tricolor displaying very wide yellow inner triad rings and a tangerine phase sibling.
(right) Same tricolor above left. Photo taken without flash.

(above) Very high ring-count amel specimen with tangerine rings that are barely distinguishable from one another.
(below) A clutch of variable tricolor amelanistics.

After these tri-colored amels started being bred by Brian, Louis and other herpetoculturists who acquired them, these breeders started introducing them into the "tangerine" phase bloodlines. These snakes commanded a higher price than the original amel tri-colors did. Terry Dunham (of Albino Tricolors), Luis Torres, Dave Doherty and a father and son team later pooled funds to purchase Porras' entire group of amelanistics and hets to further popularize these snakes into the hobby. Everyone's goal was to not only produce more colorful amels, but to also breed them into the anerythristics and hypos to produce never before seen multi-gene combinations.

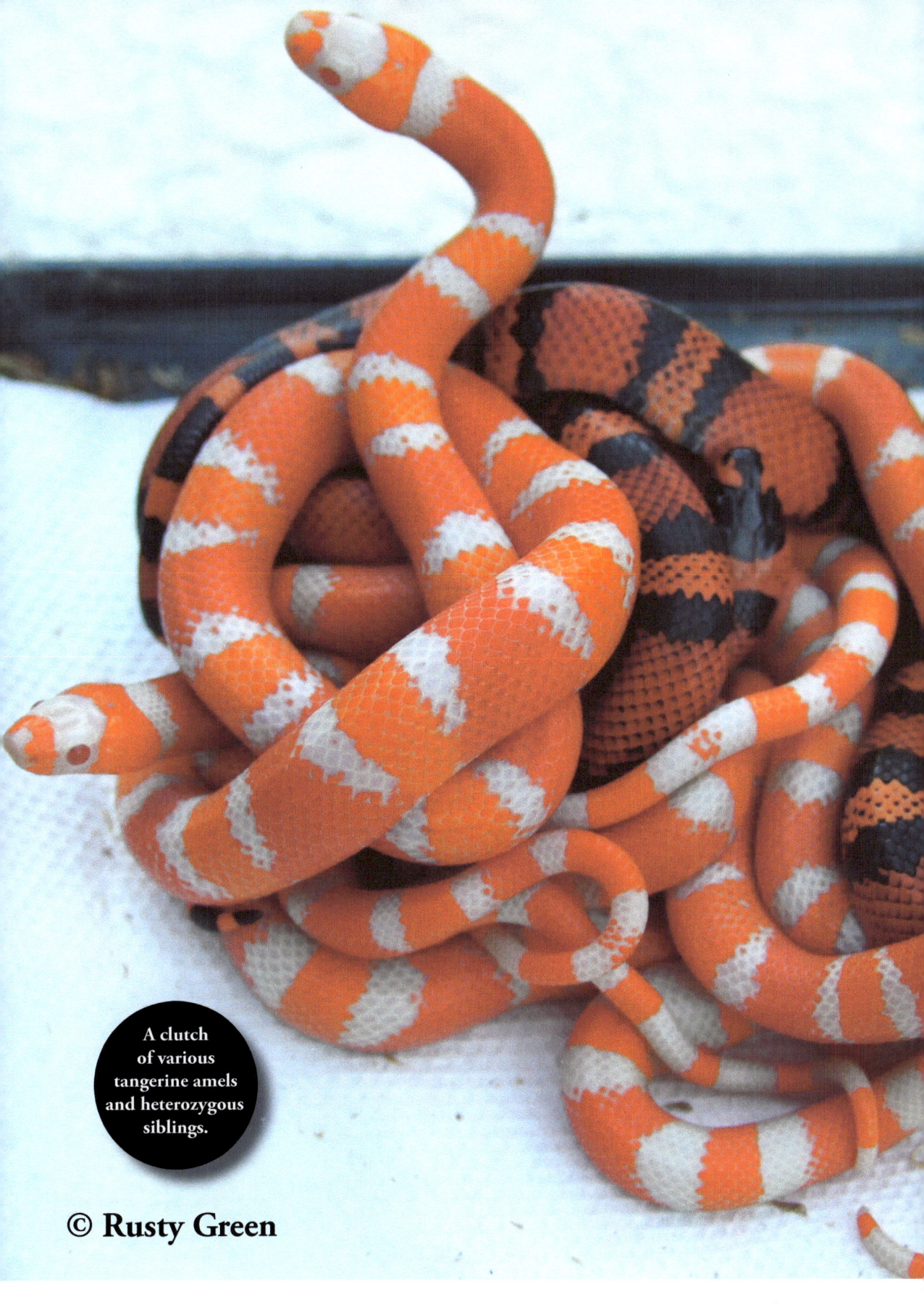

A clutch of various tangerine amels and heterozygous siblings.

© Rusty Green

A nicely colored tricolor amelanistic.

A typical tangerine amelanistic.

A group of amelanistics from some of Louis Porras' original offspring.

A typical tangerine amelanistic.

A very contrasting clean white-ringed amelanistic specimen.

Good example of carotenoid retention in this yellow amelanistic tricolor.

A specimen displaying substantial yellow scale tipping.

A large adult amelanistic breeder.

A very pale white-ringed specimen.

A very richly colored tangerine that also displays substantial yellow pigment.

An extremely yellow amelanistic specimen. This is a prime example of pronounced carotenoid retention in the xanthophore pigment cells as certain amelanistics mature. Note that the inner white rings are completely obliterated with yellow pigment.

A Collective History of Honduran Milksnakes for the Hobbyist

Anerythristic

Anerythristic (anery) means "pertaining to absence of red pigmentation (erythrin). These snakes only display their normal dark pigments, and are essentially black and gray to pinkish-gray and white animals. Normal phenotypes will typically develop black tipping as they mature and so will these. Many of these snakes don't quite seem to have a *total* absence of red pigmentation. This is due to the combinations of yellows and red pigments.

The term "xanthic" means pertaining to yellow, and is derived from the Greek word "xanthos". Xanthophores produce both red and yellow pigments known as pteridines. These can vary in color from pure yellow to pure red, or any intermediate shade in between. Xanthophores that possess a predominantly red coloration are referred to as erythrophores. Therefore, the distinction between these two types of pigment cells (chromatophores) and the specific coloration of pigments each are capable of producing is not always clear. Different shades of orange are a perfect example of this, since orange is a varying combination of yellow and red. When snakes that would normally consist of different shades of orange are completely missing only the red, but leaves the yellow, the term anerythristic would best apply. If both the red and yellow pigments are completely absent in a snake that would normally display the two colors, then "axanthic" would be the most accurate term.

If red and yellow were then greatly reduced, the term "hypoxanthic" would be the proper term. In certain circumstances, with some of the different types of snakes in the hobby, axanthism and anerythrism could be thought of as being synonymous with one another, but certainly not always.

A perfect example of when the term "anerythristic" would not apply correctly would be with the axanthic Desert Kingsnake (*L.g.splendida*) mutation in which they are completely missing all traces of their normal yellow pigment. These and other similar looking snakes in the hobby are sometimes referred to as "anerythristics", and vice-versa. Since their normal natural color scheme never involves red at all, and only yellow, the term anerythristic cannot be applied to these snakes. These black and pure white forms of Desert Kingsnakes are clearly axanthic, and not anerythristic.

Xanthophore cells are also known to retain yellow to reddish pigments that are contained in the diet of snakes in the form of carotenoids. This carotenoid retention continues throughout the life of the snake. The pigment intensity can vary based on the types and quantity of the carotenoids contained in their diet. An individual snake or a particular bloodline's genetic predisposition for storing these can also greatly affect their appearance. This is what is likely responsible for the yellow coloration intensifying in certain amelanistics as they mature. Another example of possible carotenoid retention is with the snow mutation. When they age their yellows and pinks occasionally intensify.

Flamingos also do this, which is how they acquire their pink coloration. Other animals such as certain shark species that feed largely on crustaceans are also known to develop golden yellow and pink colorations.

While we are on the subject of pigments, this will be a good time to address the issue of the inner light triad rings of the "anerythristic" morph. These inner triad rings are always white in the anerythristic forms of these snakes.

A Collective History of Honduran Milksnakes for the Hobbyist

A typically colored very high ring-count anerythristic specimen.

Oddly enough, these rings never display any hues of pink, yellow or orange as one might expect to see sometimes. The fact that there are thousands of tangerine phase and red bicolored Honduran Milksnakes in the hobby, wouldn't it be expected to see coloration other than white within these rings? We know when you breed a tangerine phase to a tangerine phase; the offspring would typically be tangerine most of the time, and slight variations of orange or red. If you breed a tangerine heterozygous anerythristic to a tangerine heterozygous anerythristic, wouldn't you expect the anerythristic offspring to display a pinkish grey hue in the inner triad rings, as well as the red body rings? Maybe some of this could be due to how the cells in the inner rings are actually structured compared to the other rings. They may refract and reflect the spectrum of light differently back through the pigment layers that our eyes perceive as being pure white.

Cells known as "iridophores" play a very key role in how white, blue, and green color is perceived by the human eye. There are no such pigment cells (chromatophores) that produce these actual colors. The crystalline structures of the iridophores themselves are what causes light spectrum to reflect back. This causes them to "seem" blue, green, white, and reflective silver to our eyes, similar to a mirror's surface. Animals such as certain fish, squid, lizards and other living things can actually manipulate these refractile platelets through their intricate muscle contractions. Iridophores are also what gives Iguanas, Emerald Tree Boas, Green Tree Pythons, Chameleons and other animals their green or blue coloration. The light is reflected in a prism fashion as it passes back through the yellow xanthophore layer towards the scales upper surface. These reflective platelets are comprised of uric acid based components called purines. There needs to be more scientific studies done in order to better understand the complex dynamics of reptile pigments.

With all the inconsistencies throughout the hobby regarding genetics and its terminology, hobbyists need to understand which terms best describe certain mutations. The marketing terminologies for many of these do not always accurately correspond with what they are. For example, anerythristic Honduran Milksnakes are probably best described as hypoerythristics.

This is the very first known anerythristic *L.t.hondurensis* from the late 1980s that Ernie Wagner acquired. This was an import juvenile from Honduras. (below) A very unique Honduran that is displaying a pink hue in the inner white triad rings (rings of three). This is VERY non-typical of anerythristics.

In the early 1980's, a breeder named Ernie Wagner acquired a juvenile anerythristic Honduran Milksnake, which was in fact a true *L.t.hondurensis*. Ernie states via a personal communication that he recalls this anerythristic snake being acquired through Louis Porras and Joe Baraducci of "The Shed" in Miami. He then raised it to adulthood in hopes of eventually breeding it and hopefully producing heterozygous offspring, or whatever this strange looking milk would ultimately produce. This exciting project all came to an end one day when he found her dead. Due to the marks found on her, he believes she was attacked and constricted by her cage mate. Ernie strongly suspected that this was caused by the male smelling the scent of a previously eaten rodent meal on the female snake. Another tragic part of the story is the fact she was gravid with eggs at the time.

One of the anerythristics Dave Doherty produced relatively early on.

A very clean anerythristic acquired from Brian Barczyk back in 1996-97 as a tiny hatchling.

A slightly aberrant specimen produced from the sire in the above right photo.

Then around 1987-1988 a collector in Honduras found an anerythristic Honduran Milksnake. This time, David Doherty acquired the mutant milksnake. He then produced hets, and in 1991 produced the very first captive-bred anerythristics available to the hobby. Brian Barczyk and Mark Bell were among the first to acquire and breed these animals from Dave, and popularized them into the hobby mainstream.

Another possible line of anerythrism popped up in 2010 when a breeder bred two snows together and produced amelanistic offspring. The story on the next page is from California breeder, Shannon Brown.

A clutch of anerythristics and normal hets produced from the same sire in top right photo. Note the variable gray-pink coloration between them.

Another one of Dave Doherty's early anerythristic offspring.

"Back in the fall of 2010, a guy contacted me asking if there was only one line of anerythristic Hondurans in the hobby. At first, I said yes, why? He said that he had a buddy of his that had bought a pair of adult snows (anery x amel) from two different people, and later bred them. His buddy hatched out 7 or 8 albinos, but not a single snow!

I asked him where the adults came from, and he said that the male was purchased on-line, and all he really knew about it was that it was from "Terry Dunham's" line. He said that the female was purchased from a table at the Tampa show, and that the seller only indicated that it was from John Lambert's line. Just as soon as he said "Lambert", I immediately remembered a conversation John and I had back in Daytona around 2004-2005. John had told me that he imported an anerythristic in from Canada (I think from Peter Rice) that "looked" way different than the other commonly seen "Dave Doherty" line that we all had in the hobby. I really didn't think anything of it until he had mentioned John Lambert's name. It was like a light bulb went off in my head! I said oh, wait a minute!, now that you mention it, I remember Lambert specifically telling me that he had a very different looking anerythristic that he bought from Canada. John said he was going to breed it into the albinos and snows, etc... That he already had. I lost contact with John, as did most everyone else when he got out of the hobby, so I never heard if he had ever done any breeding trials with it, or anything. I guess I now have the answer and it looks like he did in fact have a different strain of anerythristic.

I tried to purchase the adult pair because I was going to take the Lambert animal and breed it to some of my old-school line of L.t.hondurensis that were never out-crossed, or het for anything and try to isolate the gene to see what it looked like in its pure form. The guy told me that his buddy had sold off the adult pair before the clutch hatched, but he couldn't remember to whom because it was at a reptile show. I then tried to purchase the 7 or 8 offspring, but again, I was a little too late, and his buddy wholesaled them off as just typical albinos. He obviously didn't know that they were amelanistics that were double het for two different strains of anerythrism. Looking back on this, I am thinking this second line was probably a true anerythristic and not a greatly-reduced hypoerythristic like the common hobby line likely is, but there's no way of knowing anything about them now. Maybe one day some of these might surface again.........."

A Collective History of Honduran Milksnakes for the Hobbyist

The possible second form of anerythrism showed its rare gene once again in 2011. A long time keeper and breeder from Texas, Stu Tennyson, bred a ghost female to a snow male and produced normal phenotype, anerythristic, and what appears to be ghosts. Considering the visual genetics of the parents, none of the offspring should have been of a normal phenotype. The female being a ghost has both the anery and hypo gene, and the father being snow has both the anery and amel genes. As the offspring shows the father was also possible heterozygous for hypomelanism. All the offspring should have been anerythristic and/or ghosts heterozygous for the amelanistic gene. Further breeding trials in the next few years should prove that this may well be a second form of anerythrism.

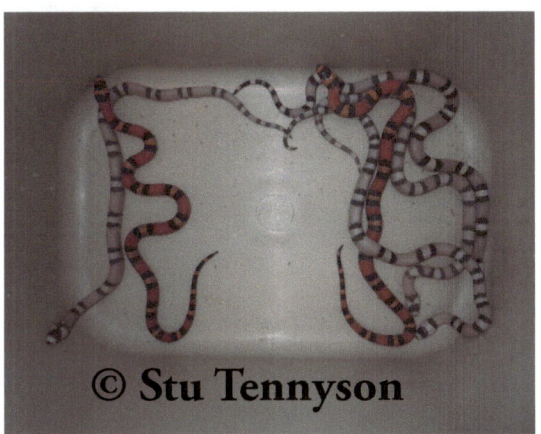

Father (top left)
Mother (top right)
Litter (middle left)
Mother with eggs (middle right)
Female Ghost; Female Ghost; Male Ghost (bottom left to right)

A Collective History of Honduran Milksnakes for the Hobbyist

Hypomelanistic

© Rusty Green

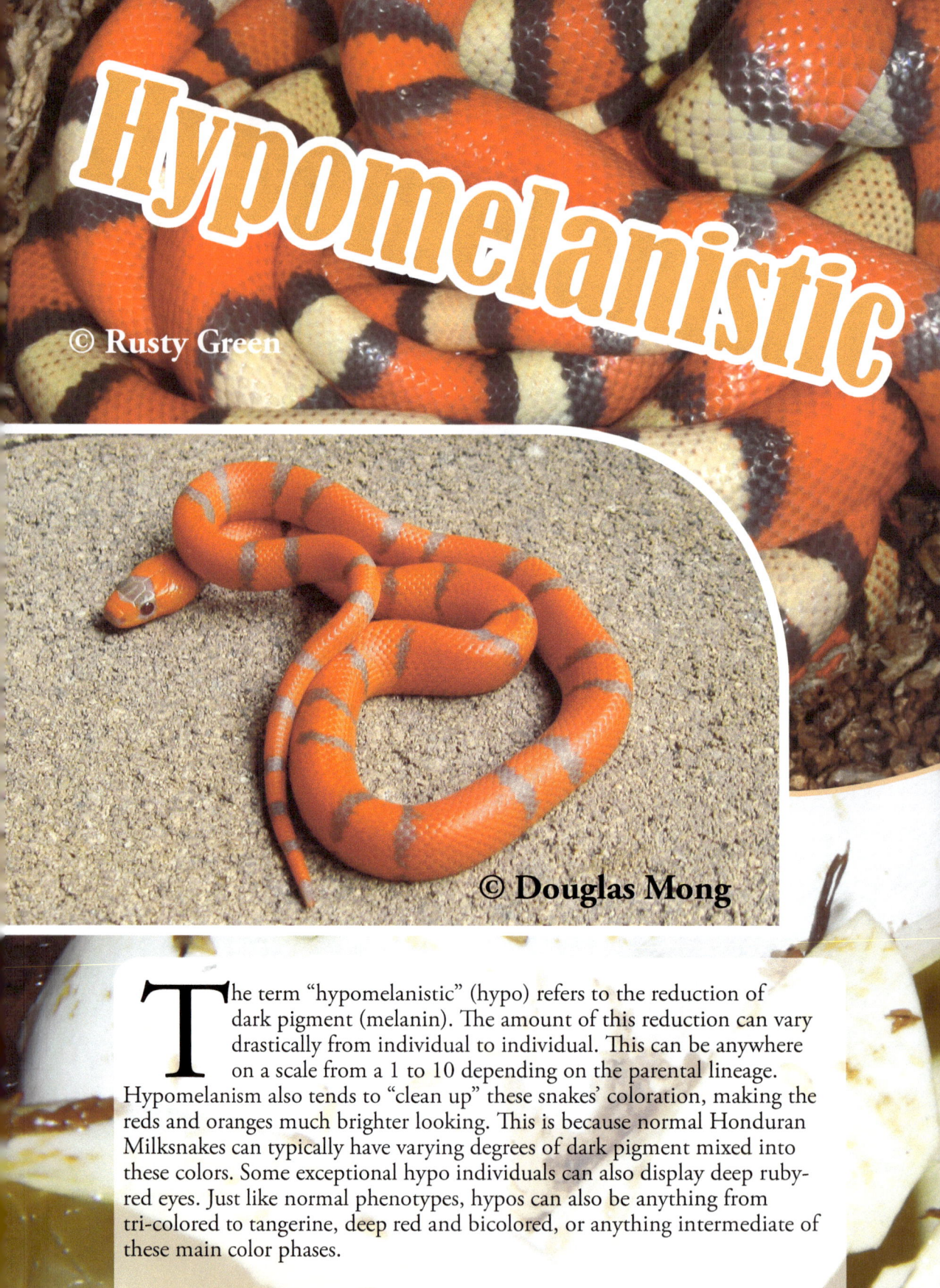

© Douglas Mong

The term "hypomelanistic" (hypo) refers to the reduction of dark pigment (melanin). The amount of this reduction can vary drastically from individual to individual. This can be anywhere on a scale from a 1 to 10 depending on the parental lineage. Hypomelanism also tends to "clean up" these snakes' coloration, making the reds and oranges much brighter looking. This is because normal Honduran Milksnakes can typically have varying degrees of dark pigment mixed into these colors. Some exceptional hypo individuals can also display deep ruby-red eyes. Just like normal phenotypes, hypos can also be anything from tri-colored to tangerine, deep red and bicolored, or anything intermediate of these main color phases.

Super Hypomelanistic produced by Steve Osborne of Professional Breeders.
© Steve Osborne

© Rusty Green

Bill and Kathy Love were the first breeders to ever produce a hypomelanistic Honduran Milksnake. In 1993, the Love's paired Honduran # 84017 with one of its offspring and hatched out two hypomelanistics that were very noticeably different and lighter than the "Tangerine Dreams" they previously produced. Apparently, the snake labeled as a "Coral Snake" in the Miami shop years prior was also heterozygous for hypomelanism!

Ironically in 1986, Steve Osborne of Profession Breeders also imported a male that was heterozygous for hypomelanism. He created and coined this strain as "Super Hypo Honduran Milksnakes". Even though it is unrelated to Bill Love's strain of hypomelanism, it was determined that both strains were compatable.

"Kathy and I bought the original 'Tangerine Dream' L. t. hondurensis for $25 from Aurora Castellanos (her Honduran import business was called Viva Animales, in Miami) around 1985-86. It was under deep shavings in a small aquarium in her narrow venomous herp room in her shop (which I asked to see because I was interested in eyelash vipers). She was convinced it was a coral snake. She said they came in as extra 'junk' that she really didn't want, and was probably tickled to 'ream' me for that much to be rid of it. I knew instantly that it was a Honduran milk; that was the only thing I ever thought it was.

After we hooked it out of the cage (because it was 'venomous') and bagged it, we moved past her hot room to look at other herps she imported from family members in Honduras. That's when my companion — renowned herp artist Marty Capron of Kansas — asked if the 'coral' I bought was what he suspected it really was, and I replied 'yes'. Marty immediately said "I wonder if there are any more of them hiding under the shavings in the cage". I was so excited to get the one I saw tucked behind the water bowl that I never checked for others in the cage. Marty uncovered one more milk – a tricolor phase baby L. t. hondurensis, which he bought for $25 also. Aurora (the store owner) didn't recognize juvenile milks for what they really were, but since she paid for corals, she made the proper mark-up on them.

We eventually bred it to other hondurensis that we got from Viva Animales and other importers who were getting hondurensis in quantity at the time. We chose the most attractive females we could find. Aurora imported only from Honduras, but I suppose it's possible even her imports (or those of numerous others) could have come from broad areas that included other races of L. triangulum."

Personal communication between Bill Love and Terry Dunham, provided by Terry Dunham

After these first hypomelanistics made it to the market place and more people started acquiring and breeding them, they started producing some of their own. Herpetoculturists soon started producing lighter hypos from these selective breedings. They were also out-crossing them into different bloodlines and morph combinations.

Mike Falcon soon pushed melanin reduction to the limit with the first "extreme" hypo in 2001. These snakes' outer triad rings were reduced to a silvery/gray, the lightest of any hypomelanistic to date. The extreme reduction in melanin in these snakes even reduced the eye coloration to a deep ruby red much like an amelanistic. The size of their outer triad rings can be normal and fairly wide, to reduced pin-banded. They can also be slightly or very vanished patterned.

California breeder, Shannon Brown and the co-author, Douglas Mong have chosen to classify the slightly darker versions of "extremes" as "ultra-light" hypos. For many hobbyists it can be quite difficult to distinguish between the two unless they have seen a good number of these different types for themselves.

These snakes are clean and bright in regards to their body colors, and the tangerine extremes are a fluorescent "pumpkin" orange. Some individuals can also be more of a red or red/orange coloration depending on their parental lineage. There are also tri-color versions of extreme hypos in the hobby that are being produced, but as of this writing are less commonly seen.

MEGA

Original mystery male

Mega hypo tricolor as subadult.

Mega hypo tricolor as neonate.

The story of the "Mega Hypo" begins back in 2000. Terry Dunham produced some of the first triple heterozygous Hondurans (heterozygous for hypomelanistic, hypoerythristic (aka anerythristic), and amelanistic). These "triple hets" were the offspring of a snow bred to a hypo (the ghost morph was not as common in the hobby at that time).

In 2001, Jeff Alloway purchased a trio (1.2) or two pairs, 2.2 of Terry Dunham's triple hets and quickly grew them to breeding size. In 2003, one triple het pair produced 5 eggs, unfortunately only one egg made it, but it was really different looking!

Jeff Alloway called this different looking Hondo, the "Mystery male" because it was unknown what morph he had actually produced. Some speculated that it was a Hybino (hypomelanistic and amelanistic) because of its light color, in what would normally be the "black bands".

Jeff Alloway repeated more triple het to triple het breeding in 2004 and produced another amazing looking neonate. This one was a tricolor hypo and was later sold to Shannon Brown. Around the same time, Don Shores also acquired a few of this clutch, two females, one hypo looking and the other appeared normal, at the time.

As you can see from the two photographs to the top right, the "normal" looks dramatically different that any typical "hypo". Unfortunately, this so-

called "normal" along with Shannon Brown's outstanding mega tricolor were both lost in brumation.

It is unknown what, if any additional breeding was accomplished by Jeff Alloway in 2005. However, in 2006, Jeff Alloway sold his entire collection to Terry Maheuron. In 2007 Terry continued to work with this unnamed line and produced a huge clutch of 14 eggs from breeding the "mystery male" back to his triple het mother, shown in the following photograph.

Terry Maheuron produced a huge number of morphs in this one clutch..... hypos, amels, anerys, ghosts, snows, normals and a few that looked exactly like the "mystery male" sire. Due to the

(Left) Two Mega Line animals, one "hypo looking" from Jeff Alloway and the other from Terry Maheuron's Mega line male. (Top) This female started out as a normal tricolor and turned as it aged. Sibling to the original Mega Hypo male. (Below) The matriarch of the "mega" line. Triple het female which produced the original male.

"mystery male" look being reproduced at this time, Terry Maheuron coined the morph, "Mega Hypo" to differentiate it from other known hypo lines (like Mike Falcon's "Extreme hypos"). Also, it proved the "mystery male" was at least heterozygous for amelanism and anerythrism.

Don Shores, Rusty Green, Shannon Brown and a few others all acquired animals from this clutch. Terry Maheuron, in 2008, paired the Mega male to a John Lambert line vanishing amel; the outcome

Original male Mega being bred back to his mother.

A Collective History of Honduran Milksnakes for the Hobbyist

of this pairing produced half vanishing amels and half Mega hypos. Based on these results, it is likely that this amel was directly related to the same lines that produced the original "Mystery male" (originating from Terry Dunham).

This breeding and subsequent clutch proved that the "Mystery male" was a "Mega hypo" and not a "Mega hybino" as previously thought. So in other words, the Mystery male was no longer a mystery, he was ultimately proven to be a Mega hypo het anery and het amel.

The photograph below is one of the offspring from that pairing.

Hatchlings from clutch pictured from previous page.

© Rusty Green

Later in 2008, Terry Maheuron decided to sell his entire collection of Hondurans, including the Mega line group to Don Shores. Since acquiring the Mega line collection, Don Shores has had limited success in reproducing the "Mega hypo" phenotype.

Rusty Green also produced a Mega hypo looking offspring in 2011. He bred a Mega tricolor het snow to a hypo het snow and produced one Mega tricolor out of 7 fertile eggs. The above photographs are of the Mega tricolor hypo 66% het snow.

After checking the breeding records, Rusty was able to trace back the lineage of his hypo het snow female to a triple het pair that was purchased from Terry Dunham in the early 2000's.

These hypos originated from triple het to triple het breeding. Don Shores, Shannon Brown and Rusty Green can all trace back the Mega hypo lineage directly to Terry Dunham. At this time, no other known very light gray hypo morph has been produced from normal phenotype parents (het to het breedings). However, this Mega hypo line does seem to be allelic to other common hypo genotypes.

Don Shores, Shannon Brown and Rusty Green and a few others are still working to understand this interesting morph with more breeding experiments in the future. .... It is interesting to note that many of the "Mega" line animals display heavy tipping and broken snout bands which are known characteristics of *L.t.polyzona*.

Chapter 6
Double Genetic Mutations

© Rusty Green

Ghosts

The ghost morph is a combination of two single genetic mutations, anerythrism and hypomelanism. When these two recessive genes are combined at the same time, the snakes tend to display a paler "ghostly" appearance, hence the term "ghost". Just as hypomelanistics can have varying shades of dark pigment, so can the ghosts since hypomelanism is also involved. They can have seemingly jet black pigment, or the pigment can be reduced to the point of silvery gray. These morphs can often display thinner outer triad rings too, depending on the parents and bloodline they originate from.

© Don Shores

© Shannon Brown

The main difference with ghosts is that they tend to be "cleaner" and display less scale tipping than an anerythristic. Even the much lighter and paler ghosts will display less (to no) black tipping as hatchlings. However, all ghosts will develop varying degrees of tipping as they age. The lack of dark scale tipping is more evident in their red body rings (RBR). In fact, ghosts can vary drastically depending on their particular bloodline and/or their individual genetic predisposition. Some ghosts can resemble extremely clean looking anerythristics, and they can sometimes be tough to

92 The Guide to Honduran Milksnakes

distinguish from one another, especially for the more novice hobbyist.

Unlike anerythristics, ghosts can have either a snow white inner triad ring or slightly off-white to almond. These off colored triads are usually the result of being an intermediate "peach", tangerine or bicolored phase. Generally speaking, anery's and ghosts that display much wider light inner triad rings are usually the "tangerine" forms, but this is generally speaking and isn't always the case. Combining two genetic mutations in homozygous form can sometimes make an individual mutation be displayed a little differently.

Houston veterinarian David Doherty not only produced the very first anerythristics, but also hatched the first ghost on August 5, 1999, beating California breeders Bob Montoya and Gary Keasler to it by only a week.

Ghosts

© Shannon Brown
© Douglas Mong
© Douglas Mong
© Don Shores
© Douglas Mong

Mega Ghosts

Extreme Ghosts

The first "Extreme Ghost" that Mike Falcon produced in 2005.

A slightly darker extreme ghost depicting the deep ruby-red eyes.

The same darker extreme ghost as in the above photo.

The "extreme ghosts" are similar to the genetics of the regular ghost trait (anerythristic x hypomelanistic), with the exception of having the extreme hypo gene in place of the typical hypo gene. This gives these snakes a much more faded, "bleached-out" appearance than a typical ghost. With the melanin in these snakes being reduced to this greater degree, their eyes also have a ruby-red appearance just as the extreme hypos do.

Central Florida breeder (Mike Falcon) was the first to produce an "extreme ghost" back in 2005. Since then, Joe Exposito, Don Shores, Shannon Brown and a handful of others have also produced a few. As of this writing, there are very few of these snakes known to exist in the hobby.

Hybino

Hybino is a term used for snakes that are homozygous for hypomelanistic (hypo) and amelanistic (albino). Not surprisingly, the only mutant trait that is visible to the eye is the amelanistic part. This is because the amelanistic gene will always "mask" the hypo gene. If you think about this, how would you be able to see a reduction of a color in the complete absence of the color? The only way to truly know that a snake is a hybino is either by knowing the parental genetics, or by test breeding.

The phenotypes of hybinos aren't so relevant in themselves, but the breeding capabilities of what they can produce are crucial in making other multi-gene combinations.

Terry Dunham (formerly of Albino Tricolors) produced what was thought to likely be the first "hybino" in 2000, and it did in fact later turn out to be a proven "hybino" in 2005. Since these morphs are impossible to distinguish from typical amelanistics, before Dunham could prove the genetics of this snake out from a future test-breeding, other breeders had produced definite hybinos from hypo, het amel x hypo het amel pairings that made the identification easy. With this particular breeding combination, any amelanistic produced would then automatically be a hybino.

First known Hybino was hatched out by Robert Seib in 2005. This wasn't the first one, as it took Terry Dunham until 2005 to prove out his 2000 hatch hybino.

© Don Shores

The term "snow" refers to snakes that are visually expressing both amelanistic and anerythristic genes. When these two recessive traits are combined into one single animal, they display a very faded and pale look to them. These snakes are basically left with virtually no red/orange, yellow or black pigment. These snakes look extremely pale and bleached out with only slight traces of pattern and/or color. Some snows, especially as they mature can develop much more of this coloration. The varying shades and intensities of pinks, yellows and even greenish hues on certain individuals can be quite striking. Sometimes these colors intensify as the snake ages because of carotenoid retention.

The first "snow" was produced by Terry Dunham of Albino Tricolors back on 8/12/98 by combining both the amelanistic and anerythristic genes together. This was the first time that two color mutations were joined in homozygous form. This suggested that a snake can visually express two separate color mutations at the same time.

1998

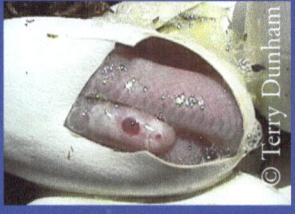

In 1998 the world saw the first snow Honduran Milksnake. This is not a mistake. After much research and along with the help of Terry Dunham, we were able to figure out that the first snow was actually produced in 1998. Most other publications portray it as 1999.

© Nathan Wells

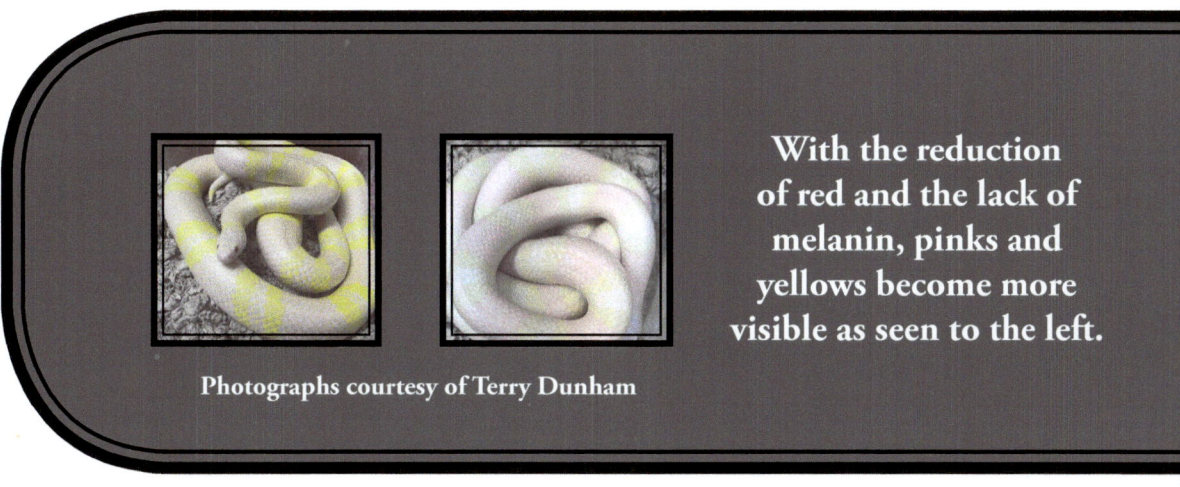

With the reduction of red and the lack of melanin, pinks and yellows become more visible as seen to the left.

Photographs courtesy of Terry Dunham

Chapter 7
Triple Genetic Mutations

The Guide to Honduran Milksnakes

© Don Shores

P earls are triple homozygous snakes that display three separate genetic traits at the same time. These recessive traits are amelanism, anerythrism, and hypomelanism. These look virtually identical to the earlier mentioned double homozygous "snow" morphs. Only these snakes have the additional hypomelanistic gene added. Just like the "hybinos", these must be proven by test breedings, or by knowing the parental genetics.

© Rusty Green

Snow and ghost

In 2009, Don Shores produced the first known triple homozygous "pearl". This was accomplished by breeding two hypos that were both heterozygous for the anerythristic and amelanistic genes. What made this pairing even far more special was that both parents were visual "extreme" hypos. Since Don first hatched this triple homozygous "pearl" that was expressing the "extreme" hypo gene, he coined this particular morph an "opal" to distinguish it in the Honduran Milksnake hobby from the "pearls" that do not express the "extreme" hypo gene.

Florida breeder, Jeff Alloway produced an animal in 2005 that might have been the very first "pearl". Alloway later sold the snake, and it was never used in any pairings that would have confirmed its genetic identity. Floridian, Rusty Green also produced a definite known "pearl" from a similar strategic breeding he carried out in 2011. Pearls and Opals are fairly rare in captive collections, but may become more available in future years.

Chapter 8
Line-Bred Mutations (polygenic inheritance)

Polygenic inheritance refers to the phenotypic characteristics that vary in different degrees, and can be attributed to the interactions between two or more genes and their environment. When more than one gene influences a trait, the inheritance pattern is not easily predictable. This best describes the genetics for the aberrant, pin-banded, striped, and/or vanishing

© Shannon Brown

© Randy Whittington

pattern Honduran Milksnakes. These traits appear fairly regularly in the hobby, but they can also vary considerably and cannot be reproduced on a consistent basis like recessive traits can. Some are apparently more consistent than others, but the least common of these are the striped and patternless individuals.

Other random aberrant patterns can also be linked to temperature fluctuations or other factors during the incubation process. These aberrant anomalies can be combined with other non-recessive line-bred traits, or any of the predictable recessive mutations in the hobby that are being covered within this book.

Herpetoculturist, Norm Damm has been a big entity within the Honduran Milksnake hobby for years. He has produced many exceptional looking specimens, including some stunning aberrant phenotypes as well. The author's would both like to take this time to sincerely thank him for all that he has contributed. However, due to time constraints at the time of this book writing, we were unable to include a few of his exceptional animals as we would have liked. We are both looking very forward to the opportunity to feature some of the outstanding snakes he has worked with and has produced in a future edition.

Bailey Line

Years ago, Marc Bailey acquired animals from Bill Love, which were from the original "Tangerine Dream" line. After breeding these animals together, an aberrant animal was produced. Marc worked with these snakes for a while before moving onto Ball Pythons. Wayne Sanders acquired some of Marc's offspring, and is continuing to refine the genetics of this line. Wayne has also introduced the amel gene into this line, and has the possibility of producing the first Bailey Line aberrant amel in 2013.

Guy Clark "Crazy Line"

Guy Clark produced one of the first fairly predictable lines of aberrant Honduran Milksnakes in the hobby. The term "predictable" meaning that the occurrences of the aberrancies were in fact somewhat predictable, but not that the particular patterns themselves are. Similar to many of the Bailey aberrant's, these snakes are also incredibly diverse and variable in their patterns, as well as their colors.

Courtesy of Jorge Sierra

European Line, aka Jaap Kooij Line

Sometime back in the mid to late 1990s Peter Rice, formerly of Rare Albino Tricolors, U.K., had acquired a tangerine female from a breeder that was located in the United States. Peter bred this female to a tricolor male, and to his surprise produced some vanishing pattern tricolor offspring.

Jaap Kooij, of the Netherlands and also Thomas Steffen, of the U.K. acquired some of the offspring from this line. Jaap then in turn, line bred these animals and produced some very clean bright colored offspring. Some of Jaap's offspring had an aberrant pattern to them. He has since sold a majority of his collection.

In 2003, Thomas Steffen acquired five individual snakes from Peter Rice; a couple of those were hypo vanishing patterned snakes. These were also heterozygous for anerythrism. In 2005, the female vanishing pattern laid her first clutch. When this clutch hatched, there were two hypo tricolor aberrant neonates. In 2010, he hatched out a ghost aberrant. Thomas is continuing to work with this bloodline. In 2010 he introduced a pearl, and plans to introduce the extreme hypo gene in 2013. Shannon Brown was able to acquire offspring from Thomas Steffen and is currently working with this line in the United States. There should be some incredible offspring being produced in years to come.

An interesting tangerine vanished aberrant constricting its prey.

© Shannon Brown

A vanished aberrant tangerine displaying odd combinations of patterning.

© Shannon Brown

© Thomas Steffen

A vanished aberrant ghost that is displaying lots of dark scale tipping as it matured more.

A Collective History of Honduran Milksnakes for the Hobbyist

Pattern Mutations

© Rusty Green

© Shannon Brown

114   The Guide to Honduran Milksnakes

Pin-banded

As the name implies, these snakes typically display much thinner rings than in the more normally patterned Honduran Milksnakes. The rings that are affected by this trait are the outer triad rings. In a normal colored and patterned snake, these are the two dark rings on either side of the middle inner ring, be it a tangerine, deep red bi-colored tangerine, or tri-colored animal. When the rings of these pin-banded snakes become so faint and dramatically reduced that they are no longer complete, they are referred to as "vanished-pattern".

© Shannon Brown

A very unique looking vanished intermediate "peach" colored hypo.

© Douglas Mong

© Douglas Mong

A vanished tangerine hypo displaying dotting remnants along the back.

A vanished pin-banded tricolor hypo.

A stunning completely vanished normal colored individual. Randy selectively bred this bloodline for 13 years to produce this incredible final product!

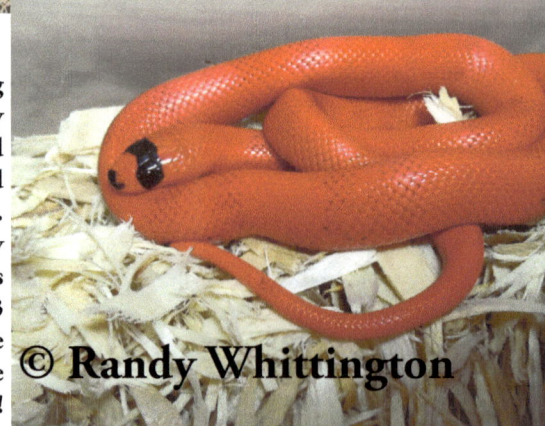

© Randy Whittington

The Guide to Honduran Milksnakes

© Don Shores

Vanishing pattern

These morphs take the pin-banded look a step further in their reduction. As the rings become more and more reduced in these types, the snakes often have the outer rings most visible on the very top of their dorsal area. Many of these have the rings gradually thinning and reducing to nothing along their lower sides. These reduced rings on the top of the back can often take the form of short narrow crossbars, or a few small incomplete spots and random flecks. Hobbyists often refer to these snakes in casual conversation, or in their classified advertisements as vanished, or simply "V/P".

Patternless

There are some individuals and bloodlines of Honduran Milksnakes that display such an exaggerated vanished pattern that it can barely or no longer be seen at all. With many of these snakes, you can still see the two alternating two-toned ring colors that would normally be bordered by these rings, while other individuals can be one solid uniform color. This is obviously only if they would be bicolored animals to begin with though. These patternless mutants are usually tangerine phase, but not always. More and more intermediates and tricolors are being bred and produced that tend to be vanished, and/or patternless phenotypes as time goes on.

© Don Shores

© Don Shores

Reverse Pattern

In 2006 Missouri breeder Chris Shulse produced a dramatic "reverse" amelanistic Honduran Milksnake. Shortly afterwards, Texas breeder Don Shores then acquired this group and was later able to produce a very small number of these very interesting looking amels over time. These incredibly unique looking pattern morphs have their body rings displayed in a bizarre "reversed" sequence. Instead of these snakes having a normal temporal band, the width is exaggerated forming what is known as a "sockhead". This is similar looking to the temporal bands of certain normal Pueblan Milksnakes (*L.t.campbelli*), or what typical Desert Kingsnakes (*L.g.splendida*) would display. Further down the body, the inner rings increase so dramatically that they become the red body rings, thus displaying their ring patterns in complete reverse!

© Don Shores

© Dell Despain

© Shannon Brown

© John Lambert

Striped Aberrant

Here is an excellent example of a "striped" aberrant that can once in a great while be produced from any of the above aberrant lines…..

Oddities

Calico

Back in 2001, breeder Steve Michaels acquired what was labeled a "Calico" and several possible hets. Before this trait could ever be established or proven out, it died along with several offspring during a power outage. This was very unfortunate, because this trait had incredible potential all by itself. The possibilities would have been endless when combined with the already established morphs available.

Burgundy

This incredibly unique looking "Burgundy" amelanistic was produced by Colorado breeder, Regis Opferman back in 1999. This snake's appearance seemed to start out fairly typical, although he did notice a somewhat odd colored scale tipping to it early on. Regis raised it up for about three more years, and noticed that it gradually developed a deep, rich burgundy coloration. He eventually decided to get out of colubrid snakes altogether, and he sold the Burgundy along with several others to another breeder in Utah.

Herpetoculturist, Shannon Brown of California also acquired some of these normal looking double-hets for hybino from this breeder. Shannon also obtained more of this bloodline from Ric Blair. Ric eventually acquired this snake and several offspring that were also produced by this Burgundy amel. All of these combined breeders never once produced anything even close to the burgundy colored phenotype of this original male. Apparently this snake was simply a very unique one-of-a-kind animal, and its color trait was never inherited. Sadly, this unique "Burgundy" male died sometime in 2007-2008 for unknown reasons.

A Collective History of Honduran Milksnakes for the Hobbyist

© X-ray by Dan Rieck of Rieck Chiropractic Center, Dunnellon, FL.
Photograph courtesy of Daniel Parker

© Daniel Parker

Two-Headed (bicephalic)

During the long incubation process, countless numbers of individual genetic codes can periodically go very wrong. Some of which can be lethal to the embryo at different stages of its development, while others can cause mild to severe deformities. Once in a great while there can be very dramatic deformities within the egg that can cause a neonate to hatch fully-developed and alive. One bizarre example of this would be a bi-cephalic (two-headed) snake.

Many times neonates that hatch with certain severe deformities do not end up living long, if at all. However, once in a great while there are two-headed snakes that do hatch and go onto lead relatively normal and healthy lives. There have been documented incidences of a few two-headed snakes found in the wild over the years, as well as a fair number of them being hatched by breeders from time to time. These snakes can also be greatly variable, with some having the heads joined close together, or some that might have separate shorter or longer distinct "V" shaped forked necks. The most desirable two-headed specimens are the rarer types that display two separate and perfectly symmetrical shaped heads and necks. A perfect example of this would be the incredible amelanistic Honduran Milksnake that Daniel Parker produced back in 2011.

Chapter 9
Record Keeping

It is very important to keep accurate, accessible records for your snakes. This can be done several different ways, either by making a personalized spreadsheet, or by using an already made program specifically designed for reptiles. These can also be made by simply sticking a categorized card to the front or lid of the enclosure they are in. This way you can record and keep track of things like:

- Feeding dates
- What type of prey was eaten?
- Shedding dates
- Brumation dates in/out
- Breeding dates (and with which snakes)
- Pre-lay shed dates
- Egg lay dates
- Number of good/bad eggs
- Hatch dates of eggs
- Outcome of clutches (what morphs/hets)
- Sex ratios of neonates
- Weight of snakes
- Growth rates
- Any possible ailments or problems, etc…

By doing this, over the course of time you will be able to notice any trends or peculiarities regarding any individual snakes in your collection that you may need to pay closer attention to. In turn, you will be able to better anticipate and adjust their individual husbandry if needed. By keeping accurate records, you can also easily calculate the cost of rodents and any other expenses too.

A general rule of thumb when keeping records for reptiles would be:

- The system should be as simplified as possible, while still allowing for maximum detail to be recorded.
- All information should be as accurate as possible. Meaning the given information should be recorded at the time they occur, or as close to that as possible.
- The system should be easy to use and time efficient.
- The system used should be open-ended so it can allow for any number of reptiles, time frames or amount of data to be added.
- The system should be standardized and able to be used on any potential species (for example, any type of reptile).

While there are many methods of keeping records, there should always be a 'hard' (printed) copy, even if a computer is the primary storage site. The use of technology to record information (for example cameras and photos), by storing it on the computer is often far easier and more efficient than using pen and paper (writing and drawing).

In the long term, this also aids in recall and later use of any information. It is recommended that you keep a backup, and update it regularly. It is also advisable to store it in another location in case of theft, fire, flood, or whatever else might possibly happen.

The record system itself, typically will involve giving every animal an identification of some kind. While it may be nice to give every pet snake a human-like name, most people with more than ten specimens tend not to do this. Therefore, the only logical way to give each animal a name is with numbers, letters or combinations of these. All major breeders, zoos and other institutions do this.

For hobbyists and/or institutions with large collections where it may not be possible to remember a number assigned to a given animal, these simple card files are often a preferred method of day-to-day use. A card (or cards) are assigned to a given reptile and stay with the reptile while in use. If or when the reptile is moved from cage to cage, the card goes right along with it.

The card is stored on the side, on top, or underneath the cage as long as it is readily accessible. Such records are particularly important in large collections where a keeper may not be intimately familiar with a given reptile. Individual animal files tend to record key data for that reptile, including body measurements at regular intervals, feedings, sheddings, and other pertinent events. Breeding activity often includes more than one reptile, so these records are often stored on different files.

Two main objectives in keeping records are to: 1), minimize time taken to do the task, and 2), to store as much needed information as possible. These two goals allow you to apply the codes and abbreviations to help achieve both. Rather than writing out full words or sentences, it is much easier and simplified to write just one, or a few letters. Many keepers have used this type of method after finding themselves spending too much time trying to maintain accurate records. The codes used are based on the words abbreviated. After using this method for only a short while, you will begin to associate them instantly and it will become second-nature.

You can also apply color-coded marks to certain card areas by using highlight markers and/or little colored stickers bought at office supply stores. These items can also be found in just about any stationery section of your local department or drug store. Using color codes for some of these more frequently marked card spaces allows for instant recognition and can be very time efficient. These records should go with any snake that you are selling, and this will alleviate a lot of questions from the buyer later on. No matter what system you choose, just remember it is important to keep these records as accurate and up to date as possible.

© Rusty Green

Examples of Common Abbreviations

Abbreviation	Description
FE	Feedings
IS	In Shed
SH	Sheddings
BRU	Brumation (date)
BR	Breeding(s)
GL	Gestation Length
PLS	Pre-Lay Shed
LD	Lay Date
NOE	Number of Eggs
FTL	Fertile
INF	Infertile
DOI	Duration/Days of Incubation
HD	Hatch Date
SR	Sex Ratio (males to females, for example 4.5)
HL	Hatchling Length (total length)
HW	Hatchling Weight (in grams)
MAO	Measurements as of (day - month - year)
STV	Snout to Vent Length
TL	Tail Length
TBL	Total Body Length (from tip of snout to end of tail)
WGT	Weight (in grams)
MG	Maximum Girth (at mid-body)
NG	No Growth (since previous recorded measurement)
P	Pinkie
F	Fuzzy
H	Hopper
M	Mouse

Chapter 10
Taxonomy

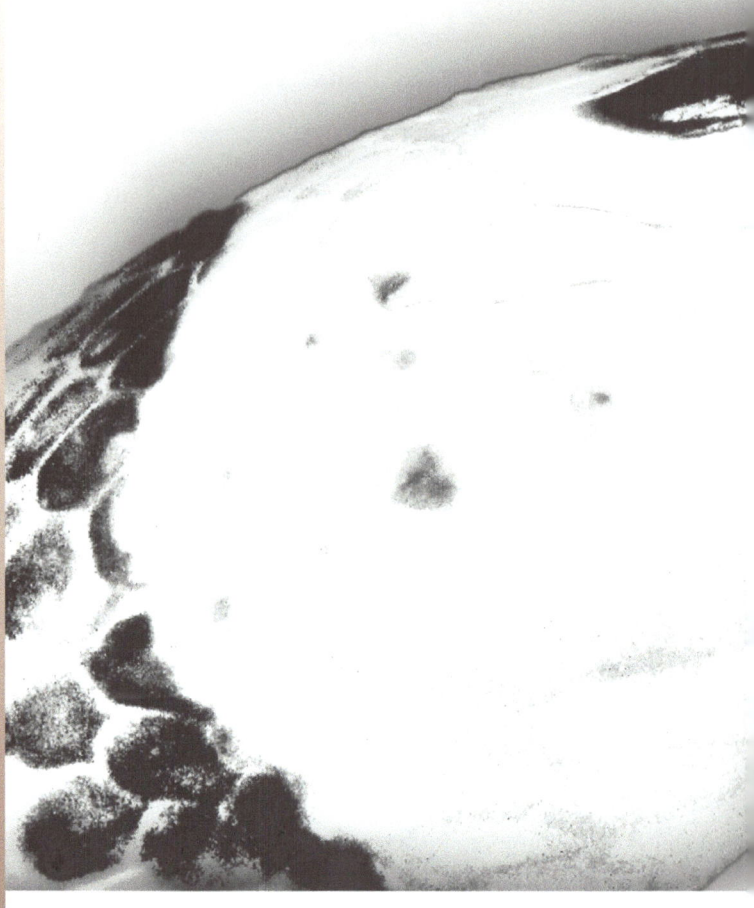

Taxonomy is the systematic classification of all known plants and animals of the world. Each species belongs to a genus, then each genus to a family and so on through order, class, phylum and kingdom. Associations within the hierarchy reflect evolutionary relationships, which are deduced typically from morphological and physiological similarities between species. For example, species in the same genus are more closely related and more alike than species that are in different genera within the same family.

Carolus Linnaeus, an 18th-century Swedish botanist devised the system of binomial nomenclature used for naming species in the mid-1700s. In this system, each species is given

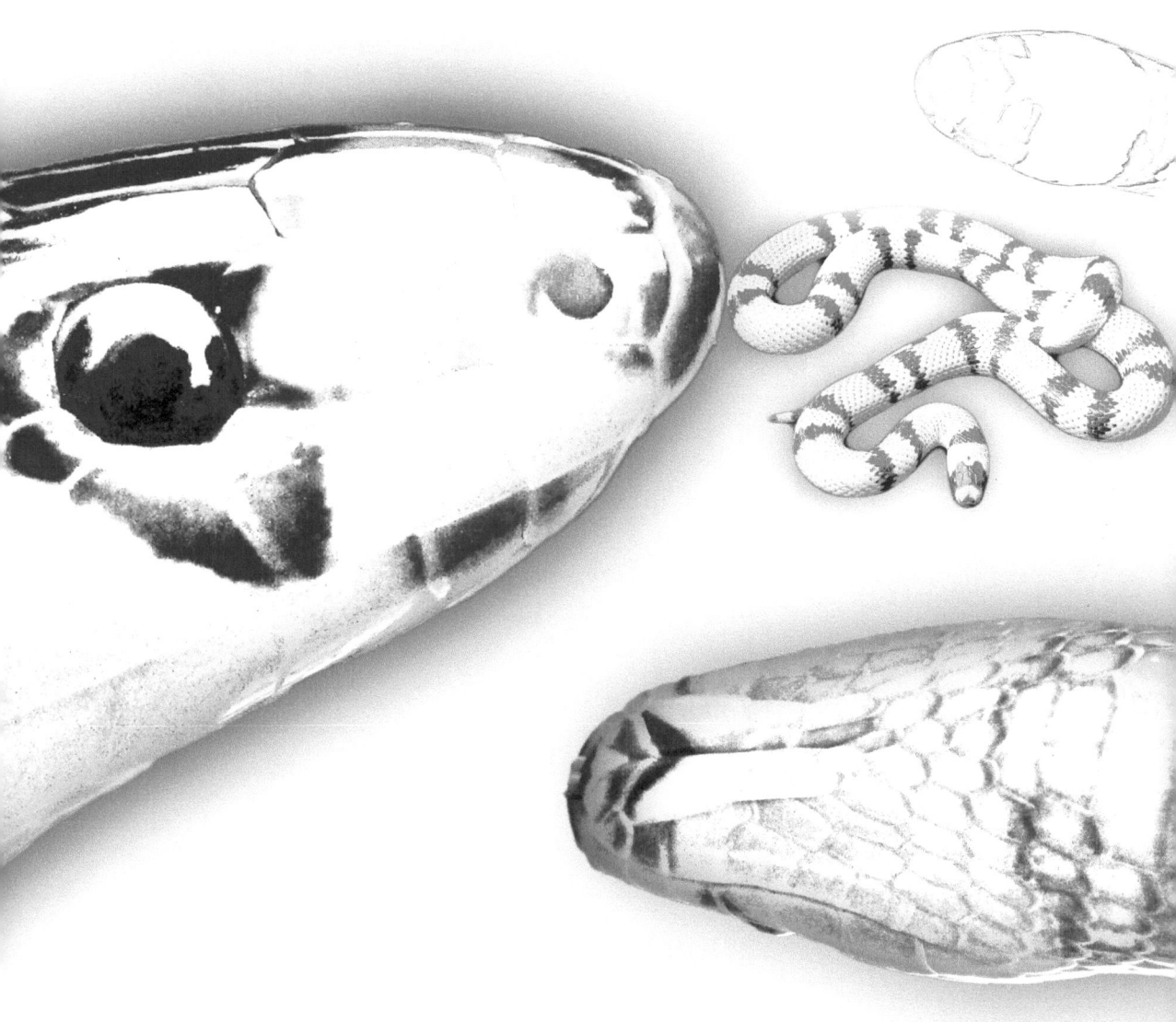

a two-part Latin name that is formed by appending a specific epithet to the genus name. By convention, the genus name is capitalized, and both the genus name and specific epithet are italicized. The Eastern Milksnake (*Lampropeltis triangulum triangulum*) is the chosen nominate race of milksnake. Therefore, the other remaining 24 recognized milksnakes are classified as subspecies of the Eastern milksnake.

Modern taxonomy is currently in flux, and certain aspects of classification are continuously being refined and subjected to change. So as mentioned, there are currently 25 recognized subspecies of milksnakes. The table below shows the traditional classification of a Honduran Milksnake (*Lampropeltis triangulum hondurensis*).

The first word of their scientific genus name "*Lampropeltis*" is of Greek origin (*Lampros*), and translates to literally mean "shiny shield", or "shiny scale". The second part of the word, (*peltis*) refers to the skin or "pelt". So when all combined, this translates to "shiny shielded skin". The following species name "*triangulum*" refers to the three colors of their triads, and the last subspecies name "*hondurensis*" refers to the snake's place of origin in Honduras.

A Collective History of Honduran Milksnakes for the Hobbyist

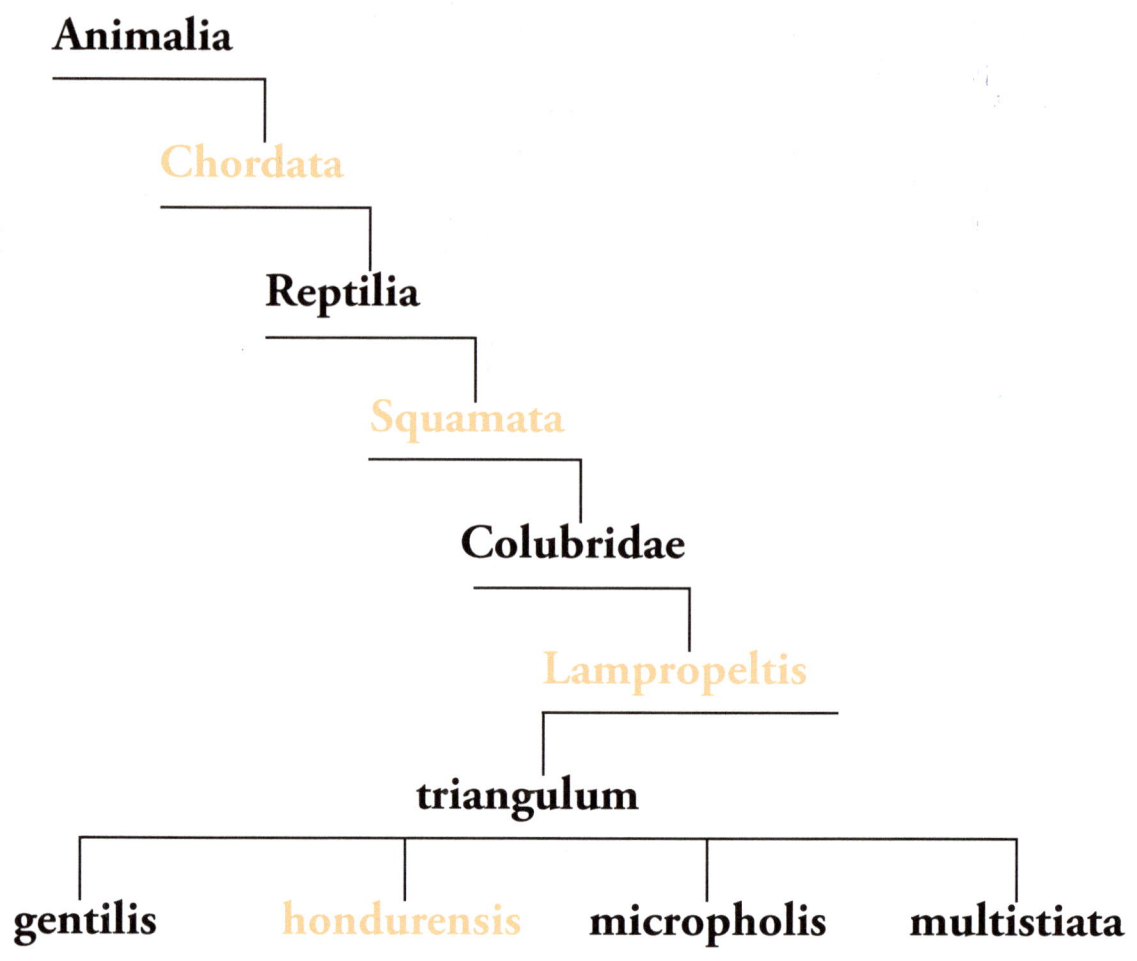

Meristics

The term "meristics" is derived from the Greek word "*meristos*" and refers to the relating to, or the dividing into segments, or organization of body structures. In relation to the milksnakes, this would include the different individual scales of their bodies and the numbers of these different types of scales on the snake's body. It also pertains to the unique markings and/or patterning of each subspecies compared to one another.

Each and every type of scale on the snake's body has a designated name that has a very specific meaning in regards to its location on the snake's body. With some of these scales, the number of them can vary and/or overlap in several of the milksnake subspecies.

Description of *L.t.hondurensis* referenced from 53 specimens examined by Kenneth L. Williams; (*Systematics and Natural History of the American Milk Snake, Lampropeltis triangulum*; Milwaukee Public Museum, 1988)

"Tangerine Dream"
© Paula Cummings

The snout has a broad yellowish to orange band that reaches to the posterior border of the internasals and most of the prefrontals. The remainder of the head is black to the posterior one-fourth of the parietals. The first yellow ring (temporal band) usually involves the posterior one-fourth of the parietals and usually extends more than one scale length onto the body (as many as four). This first light temporal ring (band) extends posteriorly to just behind the angle of the jaw. The scales in this temporal band are slightly or not at all tipped with black pigment, but there are exceptions to this in the vicinity of Tela, Honduras. The light rings vary from one and one-half to three scales in length. The first black ring begins one and one-half or more scale lengths posterior to the parietals. The first black ring is usually broadly complete across the throat. The dorsal black rings vary from two to three scales in length. The red body ring scales lack black pigment, or are slightly tipped with black. The first red ring varies from six and one-half to fifteen scales in length (mean 11.7).

Tidbits

This photo clearly illustrates how the light reflects back an iridescent prism sheen. Not only from the natural oils underneath the scales dermal layer, but also how the individual cell orientation effects what our eyes perceive as certain colors.

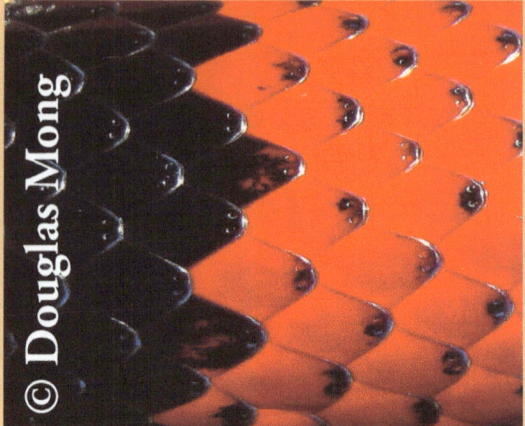

The two dots shown on the tips of each scale are known as "apical pits". It has been found that these have a large number of nerve bundles underneath the dermal surface. These are thought to be thermal sensory organs that pick up surrounding stimuli from their immediate environment, such as a predator's shadow or possible prey.

The red rings at mid-body are from five to eleven scales long. The lighter inner triad rings are slightly to moderately black tipped. The red body rings (RBR) number from 13 to 26 (mean 17.1). The temporal scales are usually 2 + 3, and the dorsal scale rows are usually 21 or 23 at mid-body. All rings around the body tend to be complete, with the light inner triad rings often being interrupted with black pigment ventrally.

This snake inhabits low to moderate elevations, with specimens being collected between 40 and 400 meters above sea level. Hatchlings are typically between 10 and 14 inches long. Adults average around 48 inches, with many attaining lengths upwards of 60 inches or more. Some specimens, although not as common can often attain greater size.

There is at least one known tangerine *L.t. hondurensis* specimen imported into the states in the late 1970s that was just shy of an incredible 8 feet long that was owned by Louis Porras. This giant *L.t. hondurensis* specimen was without question the largest milksnake of ANY kind the authors have ever seen or heard of to present date!

Anatomy

With the exception of pit vipers, pythons and certain boas that have heat sensing thermo-receptor pits, milksnakes and other colubrids sense their immediate environment with their eyes and tongue. Their eyes are very good at detecting movement, especially when the object moves erratically and is in close proximity, such as a small animal passing by foraging. However, their eyes and brains are not geared so well for identifying stationary objects without using their tongues. This is why wiggling a frozen/thawed rodent on the end of tongs initiates an instant interest and gets their tongue working. On the roof of the snakes mouth there is what's known as a Jacobson's organ. When a snake detects movement or is crawling along on the move, it will flick its tongue in and out rapidly collecting molecules from the air. These airborne scent molecules on the tongue are then drawn back and analyzed by this sensory organ and processed by the brain, thus telling the snake what it is and how to react. They can also detect vibration through the ground via the bones in their skull that alerts them to movement or impending danger.

Movement to a snake generally means one of two things. Either it is something to be very wary of and avoid, or the movement could be a possible prey item for the snake to eat. This remarkable combination of both sight and smell allows the snake to be a great time-proven survivor. This is also the reason that snakes can often be tricked into eating prey items they might not otherwise be so willing to eat voluntarily by scenting with something they do like. When the Jacobson's organ and brain specifically identify something as potential prey, then that's exactly what it is to the snake, whatever it happens to be. This is another good reason to wash your hands thoroughly after handling rodents or cleaning their bins before sticking your hand in the snake's enclosure.

© Neil Little

Typical Head Scalation

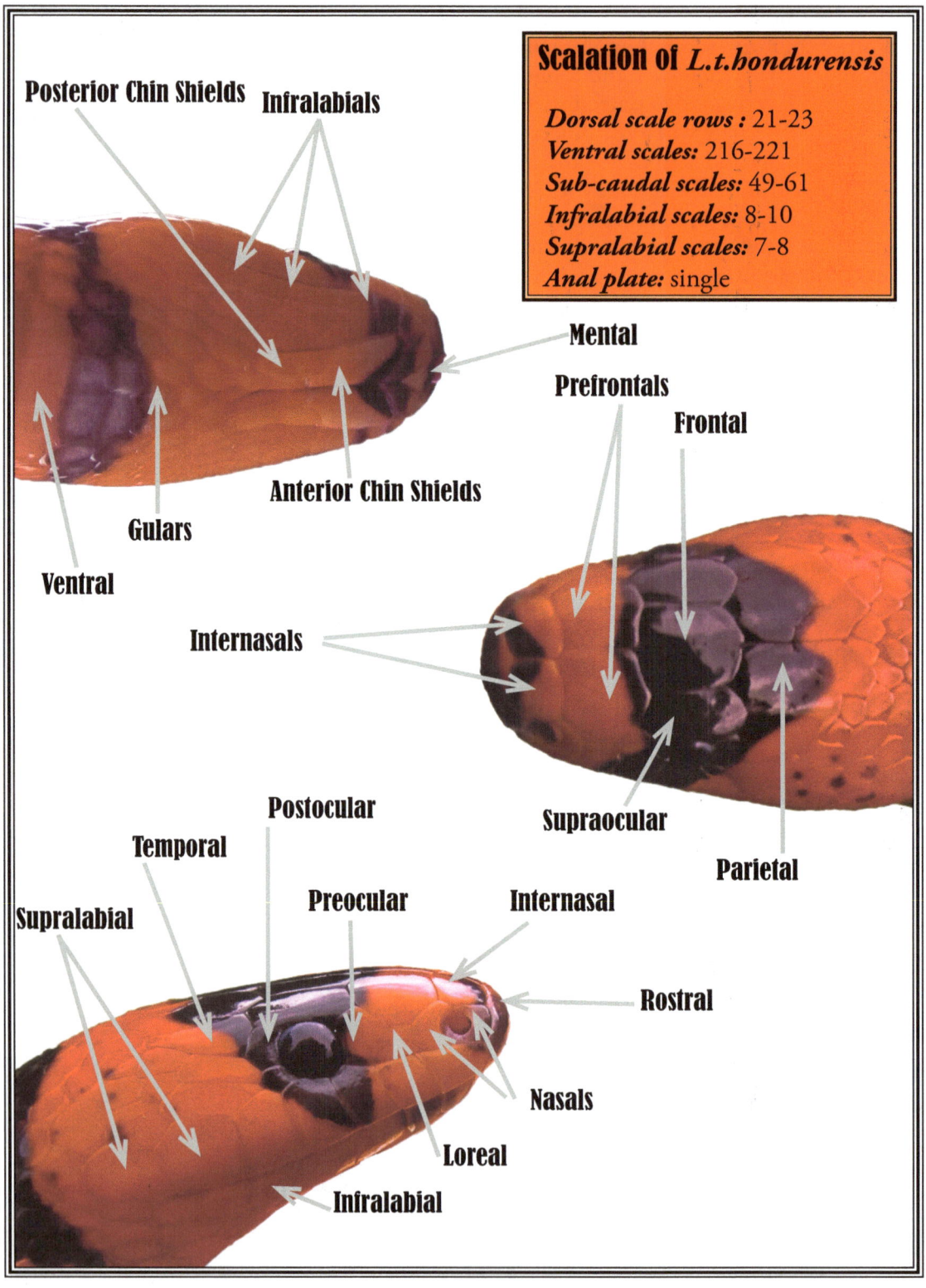

Milksnake Anatomy

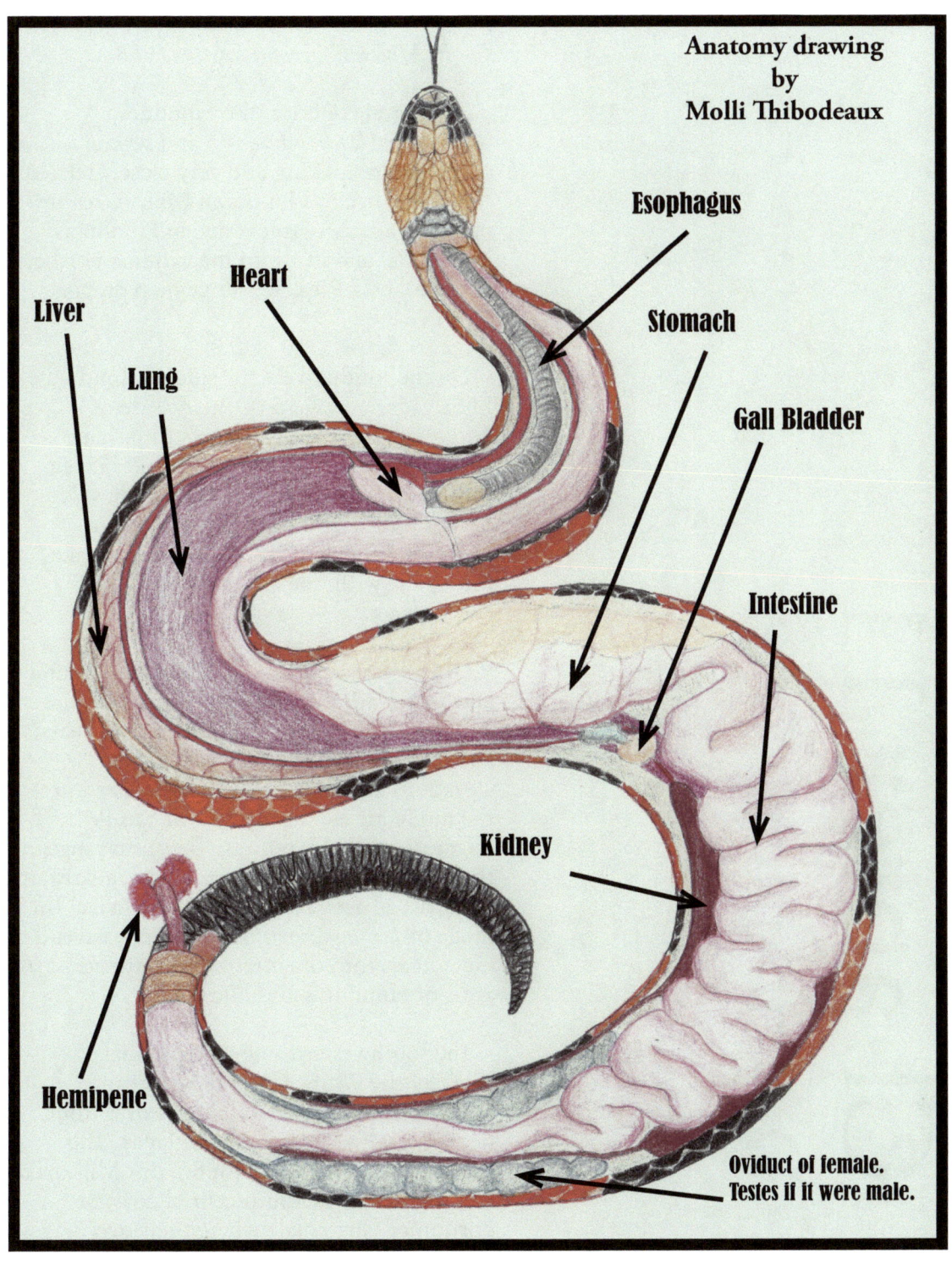

Chapter 11
Distribution

Geographic range information for these Central American milksnakes is referenced from *Systematics and Natural History of the American Milk Snake, Lampropeltis triangulum*; Kenneth L. Williams; Milwaukee Public Museum, Second Edition 1988

In Central America, the Honduran Milksnake (*L.t.hondurensis*) and several other similar looking and very closely related subspecies occur. Honduran Milksnakes are native to a rather large range in Honduras, Nicaragua, and just into the extreme northern edge of Costa Rica (see range map on pg. 141).

On the southern Pacific side of Honduras, El Salvador and western Pacific side of Nicaragua there is the Stuart's Milksnake (*L.t.stuarti*). The Stuart's Milksnakes range then continues down into the Pacific side of Costa Rica in the lowland elevations. The Honduran and the Stuart's Milksnake intergrade with one another where their ranges meet.

Directly adjacent to and west of Honduras and El Salvador is where the Guatemalan Milksnake (*L.t.abnorma*) resides. This snake's native range is in the central highland elevations of Guatemala and then east into the moderate elevations west of San Pedro Sula just inside Honduras. They also range in the higher elevations just into extreme eastern Chiapas, adjacent to central Guatemala. The range of *L.t. hondurensis* takes over eastward of Guatemala into the interior and Atlantic coast areas of Honduras and Nicaragua.

The southwestern side of Guatemala is where the Pacific Central American Milksnake (*L.t.oligozona*) ranges over from nearby eastern Oaxaca and Chiapas. This subspecies intergrades with Stuart's Milksnake (*L.t.stuarti*) in the south central coastal portion of Guatemala where their two ranges meet.

Departamento Cortes, Santa Elena, Honduras. Habitat of *L.t.hondurensis*.

The Atlantic Central American Milksnake (*L.t.polyzona*) occurs in the coastal plains and foothills of Veracruz, Mexico and up into the river valley into San Luis Potosi. It also ranges southward into the Isthmus region and broadens eastward into Tabasco, and on into northern Guatemala across Peten and La Libertad, and into the Toledo District and Stann Creek areas of Belize. Further up in northern Belize, the Blanchard's Milksnake (*L.t.blanchardi*) freely intergrades with *L.t.polyzona*. Then *L.t.blanchardi* begins to range in pure form in the territories of Quintana Roo, Yucatan, and Campeche on the Yucatan peninsula.

Provincia de Guanacaste, Costa Rica. Typical *L.t.stuarti* habitat.

© Scott Ballard

© Gerry Godin

(Upper Left) Juvenile *L.t.polyzona* from Flores / Lago de Peten, Guatemala

(Larger Picture) Adult *L.t.polyzona* from Flores / Lago de Peten, Guatemala. Produced by Scott Ballard, owned by Gerry Godin

A great example of a bicolored adult *L.t.polyzona*

© Cole Grover

© Douglas Mong

L.t.oligozona produced by Douglas Mong from a freshly imported female in 1994.

L.t.stuarti from Sardinal, Costa Rica.

© Gerry Godin

1985 *L.t.abnorma* import owned by Scott Ballard from Lago Izabal, Guatemala.

© Scott Ballard

© Douglas Mong

L.t.abnorma from the central highlands of Guatemala. Produced by Scott Ballard owned by Douglas Mong

Female *L.t.hondurensis* from Central Nicaragua

Male *L.t.hondurensis* from Central Nicaragua

Offspring from pair of Central Nicaragua *L.t.hondurensis*

140   The Guide to Honduran Milksnakes

Offspring from original imported snakes. © Nathan Wells

Range of *L. t. hondurensis*

A Collective History of Honduran Milksnakes for the Hobbyist

Chapter 12
Common Diseases and Illnesses

IMPORTANT NOTE: *The information contained in this chapter is in NO WAY meant as a substitute for seeking immediate professional veterinary help.*

During the course of owning a snake(s), you may possibly encounter some problems once in a while that need to be addressed before they quickly worsen. This especially goes for snakes that have been acquired from other sources that were not taking proper care of them. This can happen quite often when the previous owner(s) have neglected the snake before eventually deciding to part with it. Many of these diseases and illnesses can be life-threatening if not taken care of as soon as possible. It is imperative that you can detect any possible issues and/or behavior that seems out of place, and address them quickly.

Special attention to housing, temperature, and maintenance procedures can help assure that your snake is as healthy as possible and to greatly minimize stress. When snakes are stress-free it allows them to carry on with their normal activity and generally helps to insure a good feeding response. Any new snakes that are acquired should always be quarantined for a minimum two to three month period. They should be kept far away from any other animals with only the essential hide box, clean substrate, optimum temperatures and water bowl. The following are some of the common problems that can occur with captive snakes.

Egg retention: (dystocia)

Palpation

If there is a problem with your female retaining her eggs much longer than normal, the snake should be immediately taken to a qualified reptile vet for help. A commonly used hormonal drug used to facilitate in this process is oxytocin. This drug is used to induce muscle contractions. It has been noted that oxytocin is somewhat less effective on snakes than it is on turtles and lizards. It has certainly been known to help out many snakes with this condition, especially when administered early. The vet can also help with gently irrigating into the cloacal opening, and between the eggs and oviduct lining with a sterile saline solution. After doing this, the idea is to very carefully palpate the eggs out if they are freed from the oviduct wall. The oviduct membrane is very thin and delicate, so extreme care must be taken to prevent any possible prolapse and/or tearing.

Aspiration

Another common treatment for dystocia involves inserting a large-gauge needle into the egg and aspirating the contents from between the snake's ribs. When this is done, the needle and outer surface of the snake should be thoroughly sterilized.

Oxytocin may be used to start contractions if they do not start on their own within a few hours or within 24-48 hours. Caution must be taken to not allow any of the egg contents to escape and leak into the female's body cavity, as this can cause serious problems regarding infection. Aspiration must usually be done within a 48 hour period after natural laying attempts. After this short time, the contents of the eggs themselves can often begin to harden more, making aspiration difficult, or even impossible. If the eggs are not expelled within 48 hours of aspiration, they must be surgically removed by a qualified veterinarian.

Surgery

If other attempts at inducing her egg-laying have not been successful up to this point, the snake will have to be anesthetized for the eggs to be surgically removed. Before this is done however, a final attempt at manually manipulating the eggs may be tried again due to the relaxation of the oviductal muscles from the anesthesia. As mentioned previously, extreme care must be used to prevent a prolapse or rupture when gently coaxing the eggs out the vent. Depending on what is found by the veterinary surgeon, the eggs themselves, a portion or all the reproductive tissues may have to be removed. Depending on what was actually discovered and performed, it is an important judgment call as to whether the female will be in a sound enough condition to ever be bred again. Always keep the female's future health and well-being in mind when considering this. If there is any question as to her not being able to do so safely, it isn't worth jeopardizing her life.

Mouth Rot (infectious or ulcerative stomatitis)

This disease is not very commonly seen in milksnakes. However, when snakes are kept in unsanitary conditions and improper temperatures, this greatly raises the likelihood of them contracting illnesses. This disease can often be accompanied with respiratory infections as well, and vice-versa. Stress can lower the snake's metabolism allowing this disease (or diseases) to take a strong-hold and send them spiraling downhill in a hurry. By the time this happens, the snakes typically refuse to feed, which only makes things worse.

This is a very serious disease that should be treated by competent veterinarians, or at least by very experienced snake keepers. If it is not a severe case, this can generally clear up surprisingly well when diligently addressed and taken care of on a daily regimen. If you feel the least bit unable or uncomfortable about treating the snake yourself, then the snake should be taken to a qualified reptile vet immediately for treatment so its chances of a swift and full recovery are greatly increased.

The earlier signs of mouth-rot would be small darkish red dots along the gum tissue that would otherwise look uniformly whitish-pink. This can often be accompanied by a slight discharge of mucus. Under closer inspection, the snake will often not be able to fully close the mouth. This will certainly stress the snake more, and when left untreated will make matters worse. Eventually, the mouth tissue will develop a "cheesy" look to it along the snake's tooth and gum line. This can be fatal if not treated immediately, but if caught early enough, the snake can make a healthy recovery.

Typical treatment procedures

Step 1

Gently pry the snake's mouth open with a blunt flat instrument. Then gently turn it sideways to "prop" the snake's mouth open so you can work on it. Have someone else hold the snake's body and rear portion of the snake. If you are doing this by yourself, gently hold it down on the floor with the toes of your bare foot so you can get a feel of the pressure needed to restrain the snake.

Step 2

Carefully remove all rotted tissue along with any loose teeth with a pair of tweezers.

Step 3

Turn the snakes head just a bit sideways and down. Rinse the mouth well with full-strength 2 or 3% hydrogen peroxide. You can also use Betadine, or add some to the hydrogen peroxide which works well too. The Betadine will stain the dead tissue to help identify any bad areas that still need to be removed. You can draw this up in a syringe and administer it to any infected areas. It's very important to remember when you are tilting the snake's mouth to the side, that you also tilt the head slightly downward when rinsing with the solution. This helps get everything rinsed out of the mouth, and prevents any solution from going down the glottis.

Step 4

Do this at least twice a day, every single day and you should immediately start to notice a difference within several days. Keep doing this for at least another week or so until you can clearly see that the snake's mouth is healing up and is uniformly whitish-pink again. You will know if this was all successful when the snake can fully close its mouth again and resumes feeding.

Keep in mind; it is extremely important to take note if the snake has a secondary respiratory infection (see respiratory infections). This can be quite common to have two problems going on at the same time. Either one of which will usually prevent the snake from feeding voluntarily. The first thing to do is warm the snake into the upper 80s and seek veterinary help immediately for the correct type of antibiotics. The right antibiotics will properly target the infection after a bacteria culture of the saliva has been performed. The vet will know which antibiotic(s) will best target the specific type of bacteria. Remember to closely monitor the enclosure temperature with an accurate thermometer where the snakes belly is to prevent the snake from overheating. It is very important to never assume what these temperatures are.

Respiratory infections

Respiratory infections commonly referred to as "R.I." can be caused by a number of things, or combination of any of these.

- Temperatures are too cool
- Spilled water bowl in substrate (excessive humidity/mildew from not being changed)
- Not enough enclosure ventilation
- Secondary infection in conjunction with Mouth Rot (as mentioned earlier)
- Feces and urates in the water bowl, and/or enclosure from not being properly maintained.

The typical signs of respiratory infections in snakes are that they often make wheezing, "clicking", "ticking", or "popping" noises as they breathe in and out. They are often very lethargic and refuse to feed when this occurs. In its more advanced stages, they can also display some mucous discharge from the mouth, or have bubbles coming from the mouth and/or nostrils while leaving their mouths gaped open. Preferably this can be caught in its early stages and will be easier to treat and cure than if left ignored hoping it will get better on its own. These infections can be quite serious for snakes because they only have one functioning right lung.

If you see any of these signs then it is imperative that you get the snake to a qualified reptile vet for immediate attention and diagnosis. In the meantime until it can be seen by the vet, the snake should be placed in a smaller enclosure with accurately monitored temperatures of about 85 to 89 degrees Fahrenheit. This allows the snake's natural metabolism to be raised to help begin fighting the infection prior to the vet visit. The vet will typically listen to its breathing with a stethoscope for any of the above mentioned noises, and will usually take a swab smear of the mouth and throat to perform what is known as a "sensitivity culture". They will do this to see which type of antibiotics work best against the particular strain of bacteria.

Ignoring these signs can waste precious time for your snake, so taking swift action here can literally mean the difference between life and death for your snake. Amikacin, Baytril, Ciprofloxacin, and Gentamicin are just a few antibiotics that have been used successfully for combating respiratory infections in snakes.

Dosages of several standard reptile antibiotics

1. Amikacin: 5 mg/kg, IM, first dose, then 2.5 mg/kg every 72 hrs. for 5 injections (potentially nephrotoxic so animal should be well hydrated)
2. Baytril: 5 mg/kg IM/PO every 24 hrs. for at least 5 injections (in different areas)
3. Ciprofloxacin: 10 mg/kg, PO, every 48-72 hrs. (must be mixed with distilled water)
4. Gentamicin: 2.5 mg/kg IM every 72 hrs. for 5 injections (potentially nephrotoxic so animal should be well hydrated)

Internal Parasites: (endoparasites)

Worms: (nematodes, cestodes, and trematodes)

There are many different types of worms or flukes that can be present in reptiles, especially in many wild-caught animals. Fortunately, the vast majority of captive-bred milksnakes are generally not adversely affected by many of these parasites due to their captive-born environment and diet. However, once in a while there can be serious issues arise that must be addressed regarding these parasites.

These parasitic worms can come from a number of sources and be transferred to the host snake. Rodents can commonly harbor internal pinworms. Other prey, such as other snakes and lizards can often have different types of worms and other parasites. Snakes can naturally harbor some of these worms, and there is generally never much of an issue, as their natural metabolic defenses usually keep them in check. However, when the snake is stressed for prolonged periods from any number of reasons, usually due to the keeper's poor husbandry, they can sometimes multiply to a very serious level.

Symptoms

- poor appetite
- weight loss
- regurgitation
- abnormal appearing stools
- diarrhea

When these symptoms occur, the snake should immediately be brought to a qualified vet for diagnosis and treatment. They will typically perform what is known as a "fecal floatation" and examine the slide under a microscope to see what type may be visible. They may also do a throat swab too.

Treatment

Panacur: (Fenbendazole)
Panacur treats - pinworms, hookworms, hepatic worms, roundworms, strongyles, and pentastomida.

Panacur can typically be found packaged for use in horses and other livestock. Herpetologists and other reptile enthusiasts have been using this product for years with great success.

Dosage:

A recommended dose of 50-100 mg/kg once every two weeks (14 days) for reptiles until a negative fecal sample is obtained. Usually takes 2-3 doses to kill their complete life cycle. Side effects from Panacur given at recommended dosages, or even slightly higher are relatively low and almost unheard of.

Other common internal parasites:

Snakes can be affected by many other types of parasites too. A few of the more commonly seen ones are

- Entamoeba invadens
- Trichomonas
- Balantidium
- Rhizopoda
- Flagellates
- Ciliates

Note: Other bacterial pathogens can typically be present due to the parasites and their associated necrosis and swelling of the digestive tract.

Symptoms of these parasites are basically the same as mentioned earlier for worms, only the symptoms are caused by a completely different type of parasitic organism. Snakes can also contract these in different ways. A very common way is from being kept in unsanitary enclosure conditions. Another example would be the snake drinking from a bowl of fouled water that got contaminated, or not changed frequently enough. Problems can also be caused by ingesting fecal matter along with a meal or water that was consumed. This is why it is extremely important to keep close tabs on their caging and clean frequently. Snakes can also acquire different parasites from the prey host. Either way, the parasite(s) can begin to take hold in the snakes gut. This is just another good reason to offer thawed frozen prey as mentioned in chapter one. Again, when these types of symptoms ever occur, it is time for an immediate trip to a qualified veterinarian for swift diagnosis and treatment.

When snakes regurgitate from internal parasitic pathogens affecting their ability to digest properly, the last thing you want to do is to feed it another meal until the problem is addressed! Feeding at this point will only lead to more regurgitations and a definite downward spiral that could easily end in death. Any further meals consumed will only putrefy within the snake's gut, and lead to a serious "domino-effect" of problems. When a snake regurgitates because it cannot properly digest, the prey literally rots inside the snake, poisoning its entire system in the process. Once is one too many times, so obviously making sure it doesn't continue is of utmost importance for the welfare of the snake.

Treatment

Flagyl: (Metronidazole)
Vets will typically want a fresh fecal sample and do a fecal-floatation here as well. Standard treatment for these parasites and bacteria are as follows..........

Experienced reptile vets will typically prescribe and administer a dose regimen of Flagyl at the rate of 25-50 mg./per kg. of body weight given orally, and another follow-up dose 10 to 14 days later. They will sometimes give you pre-loaded syringes of this medication after your initial visit to take home if you think you are capable of administering this medication safely and properly after showing you how. This is quite simple to do actually. No food should be offered until at least a good 10-14 days after the last dose so the snake has had time to replenish its vital acids, electrolytes, enzymes and gut flora before being fed again. When it is fed again after the specified time has passed, the rodents should be very small single meals. This will ensure they stay down and are properly digested. The snake simply cannot afford for this to happen anymore, or it could easily die. After several small meals are passed successfully, you can very GRADUALLY increase the size back to what it was normally eating. Just be sure that the meals are not too large, and there is a sufficient thermo-gradient in the enclosures far end for the snake to properly digest. A probiotic such as "NutriBac" can also be given with the smaller prey offerings to help ensure the prey is digested properly. This is an enzyme product that helps the snake's gut break-down and digest the meals more easily. This probiotic has offered great results in the past. This can be found many different places online.

External Parasites: (ectoparasites)

Mites:

Snake mites are tiny arthropods that feed on the blood of living snakes. A heavy infestation can cause anemia and lethargy, and even eventually kill the snake in short time if left untreated. These parasites look like tiny pin-point sized black, or sometimes dark red dots moving around on the snake. They are typically prone to concentrate around the ocular lens and gular folds. You may also spot mites on your hands after handling a snake infested with these parasites. Often the mite feces can be apparent too, especially on dark colored snakes. The mite droppings appear as tiny lighter dots or specks on the surface of the snake. Snake mites are species specific, so they will not infect you or your other pets such as dogs or cats.

While you are closely inspecting the snake for these pests, take the animal in one hand and carefully grasp all around its entire body with the other while holding a clean white cloth or paper towel. Closely inspect it after you have wiped down the snake's entire body length in one long continuous wiping motion. If you see any of these pesky critters on the wiping material or hand, you'll instantly know there is a problem that must be addressed, and FAST!

Infested snakes will often soak in their water bowl excessively in an effort to drown the mites. If you see excessive soaking, check your snake for mites as described above, or look at the water itself for dead mites as well. Make sure that you don't mistake dirt or other grit in the water for actual snake mites. If your snake has mites, these can effectively be taken care of by doing a few basic procedures. The steps that follow are proven methods for mite eradication. Although it may sometimes be possible to treat mites successfully while eliminating a step or two, this is not recommended. Doing so may result in your snake still having mites in the future because their life-cycle was not broken. These pests need to be taken care of very methodically to ensure all are killed with no more eggs to hatch to multiply all over again.

Treatment

Step 1

You will need a secure plastic tub (Rubbermaid®, Sterilite®, etc) with air holes for ventilation that your snake will fit in. You will also need some products to kill the mites. A product called Reptile Relief by Natural Chemistry™ can be used to treat the animal itself. Provent-A-Mite™ by Pro Products™ can be used to treat the enclosure. Both of these products are readily available online, and at certain pet stores that work with reptiles. Avoid using any "seat-of-the-pants" home remedies that you may have heard of, as many of those can prove harmful, or even fatal to snakes.

Step 2

Put your snake into a secure plastic tub, and spray it liberally with the Reptile Relief, coating the animal from head to tail. Be sure to carefully follow the directions on the bottle for detailed information and instructions. Allow the animal to sit for 15 to 20 minutes while all of the mites on your snake are being killed by the product. After the recommended time, rinse the snake well with clean tap water, and rinse out the tub thoroughly too. Now soak the snake again for another 15 to 20 minutes, but this time in approximately chin deep clean water. This will prevent your snake from becoming dehydrated, as the Reptile Relief works by drying out the mites. In the 30 or so minutes required to treat the animal, you can begin working on the caging.

Note: It is recommended to re-treat the animal only just as discussed above two more times, one week apart to eliminate any chance of mites re-occurring.

Step 3

Eliminating the living mites on the snake is really only half the battle. There are still many live mites (and mite eggs) in the snake's enclosure that must be eliminated to prevent a re-infestation. First, remove all cage decors (wood, hide boxes, water dishes, etc...). All of these items will need to be thoroughly cleaned in diluted bleach and water solution. This is best accomplished by soaking the items in another large tub or trash can. Make sure that no part of the items are above the water level as the mites will climb up to escape drowning, so the entire object must be totally submerged. You will need to let these items soak for at least 20 to 30 minutes. While those are soaking, remove and discard all of the substrate from your enclosure. To actually clean the cage you can use any mild cleanser, or Zoo Med Laboratories's Wipe Out #3 cage cleaner. Or even better, the Reptile Relief can be used directly on the cage surfaces. Wipe down all surfaces thoroughly, and rinse with water if you suspect any remaining residue.

To get your cage glass sparkling clean, use a non-toxic glass cleaner or rubbing alcohol. Avoid any products with strong fumes or ammonia. After all fumes have dissipated, refill the bottom of the cage with fresh substrate.

By now, your cage items should be ready for rinsing. Rinse them well with a strong jet of clean water until no evidence of bleach remains (odors, suds, etc). Letting the rinsed items dry directly in the hot sun is a great time saver and helps to dry them completely before replacing back into the enclosure.

Now you can replace any of your cage decors back into the cage EXCEPT for the water dish, which will go in last. Once the enclosure is all set up and looking good again, it is time for the Provent-A-Mite™ product. This product works fantastic, but it is strong, so do not use any more than recommended. (Read the directions on the Provent-A-Mite can for further information) Once it is thoroughly dry it is completely harmless, but in a liquid or gas form, it can be harmful. That is why you do not want the water dish or snake in the enclosure when you spray. Now spray the Provent-A-Mite™ thoroughly over the bedding and decor at a rate of about one second per square foot (that's just over a second of spray for a 10 gallon tank, or a similar-sized tub enclosure). Allow the enclosure to air out until completely dry.

Step 4

Now you can place your snake and newly-filled water dish into the completely mite-free enclosure. In the grand scheme of things, spending an hour or two on this project isn't the end of the world, but it's certainly worth avoiding the stress on you and the animal. As a result, prevention is definitely the best medicine. Luckily, the Provent-A-Mite™ will continue to protect your enclosure from mites for about a month. Keep close tabs on these pests now that you have already had an issue with them so you can take swift action if they should ever make another unwanted appearance.

Another effective and very inexpensive alternative mite treatment:

There is a product on the market called Nix® which is designed to treat human head lice and their eggs. The one characteristic that separates the Nix® method from other mite remedies is its effectiveness at killing live mites and mite eggs. All other mite remedies do not destroy mite eggs. As such, many snake keepers have found the Nix® method to be extremely effective at eradicating serious mite infestations when diluted correctly.

Dilute a 59ml bottle of Nix® with 4 liters of distilled water. Mix thoroughly until the product is evenly distributed. You can then pour it into a spray bottle and apply to snake, enclosure and cage furnishings. The best thing about this treatment is you do not have to wait for the product to dry. Repeat every 5-7 days for a total of 3 applications. Even a prominent pet store manager who sells several commercially produced mite remedies uses the Nix® method on imported snakes arriving at his store. Another huge benefit to using Nix® is its great economic value. For around $6 to $12, depending where it is bought will produce 4 liters of solution.

Shedding problems: (dysecdysis)

Your snake will periodically shed its skin, and require a certain amount of relative humidity to do this successfully. It typically takes 7-10 days after the eyes become opaque for the snake to shed. If you notice it taking longer or only a portion has sloughed, there are a few steps to help it along. If a "humid hide" is in the enclosure with the snake, this should have done the trick. However, there can be exceptions from time to time.

A good way to help things out are to place the snake in a secure container with air holes, or a cloth bag with lots of moist sphagnum moss, but not so moist it is soaked and saturated. You can also mist the snake down real well with a spray bottle of water prior to putting the snake in with the damp moss. Keep the snake in with the damp moss for at least several hours to overnight to allow the snakes skin to absorb plenty of the moisture so it can eventually slough it off successfully. If there are still a few areas on the snake that the skin didn't come completely off, you can help it along yourself. Always make certain that both eye caps and tail tip come off completely. If the eye lenses are moist enough but still attached to the eye, you can carefully and gently work a corner loose with a small pair of tweezers or similar object. If you see that it still doesn't want to come off easily, apply a small dab of mineral oil (baby oil) to the eye caps with your finger and let that soak in for a few hours.

IMPORTANT NOTE: *Under NO circumstances should a snake ever be placed in a saturated wet pillowcase, or ever have the bag placed in a shallow depth of water thinking it will be fine. What will happen is the very close thread-count of the pillowcase will become saturated with water as the snake moves around in the bag. It will absorb the water up into the material like a wick does in an oil lamp. This can prevent air from getting into the pillowcase, suffocating the snake! Unfortunately, this has already happened to many hobbyists in the past that never thought this was possible. Believe this,......it is!*

Blister Disease: aka Scale Rot (ulcerative or necrotic dermatitis, or vesicular dermatitis)

This is an ailment typically caused by excessive moisture and prolonged unsanitary caging conditions. The damp caging substrate allows for the development of bacteria and fungus to multiply very rapidly. This is why it is so important to check for spilled water bowls and to maintain clean, dry substrate bedding at all times. This excessive moisture along with any damp fecal matter can cause the snake to develop brownish-colored rotted ventral scales and raised pustules/abscesses on the body. Secondary infection with other harmful bacteria may result in septicemia and death if left untreated. The condition starts with bleeding into the scales, followed by small, round, raised areas of inflamed skin filled with pus that eventually lead to open and slow-healing sores. Treatment with antibiotics, topical antibiotic ointment, and dry hygienic conditions are essential for a healthy recovery.

Treatment

Just as with all the other diseases and illnesses mentioned in this book, a qualified reptile veterinarian should be consulted and assess the severity and nature of the problem. The first thing to be done is immediately place the snake in a dry, clean caging environment. This can either be a layer of clean newspaper, paper towels, or dry aspen in the enclosure.

The next step is to soak the snake in a povidone-iodine solution (Betadine). This solution is typically in the 10% range, and afterwards an application of Betadine topical ointment can also be applied to the affected areas. Depending on how severe the individual case is, the vet may choose to also administer an antibiotic injection. If all goes well with the treatment, you should begin to see a very noticeable improvement in the snake's condition. Any raised abscesses and brown ventral scales should begin to dry up and get better and better looking with each successive shed.

Newly hatched 2013 Vanished Pattern Tangerine

Glossary

Allele: One of two or more possible different forms of a particular gene.

Amelanistic: Lacking melanin or black pigment.

Anal plate: A modified ventral scale that covers and protects the vent. Could be one or two scales.

Anerythristic: Lacking red pigment.

Assist feed: To start a prey item into a snake's mouth and the allowing to let the snake finish.

Axanthic: Lacking yellow pigment.

Blue: Or in shed, see Opaque.

Brumate: To place an animal in Brumation.

Brumation: Cooling a snake body temperate for a period of 2-4 months in order to trigger egg production in females and sperm production in males. Brumation usually coincides with a shorter photoperiod.

Cannibalistic: An animal that feeds on others of its own kind.

Caudal: Referring to the tail.

Cloaca: The part of the intestinal tract preceding the vent.

Clutch: A group of eggs.

Codominant: (Co-Dom) A mutant gene that disrupts the normal phenotype of a snake without having a second gene on the same allele. The phenotype of a heterozygous (het) is NOT the same as a homozygous snake.

Colubrid: A snake belonging to the family Colubridae. Most common snakes are within this family. Including King Snakes, Rat Snakes, Garter Snakes, etc…

Disecdysis: Parts of old skin that haven't shed off.

Dominant: A mutant gene that disrupts the normal phenotype of a snake without having a second mutant gene on the same allele. The phenotype of a heterozygous snake is the SAME as that of a homozygous snake.

Dorsal: Referring to the top surface of the back.

Double clutch(ing): To induce a snake to lay two clutches of eggs in one season.

Double heterozygous (double het): A snake that carries two separate mutant genes, for example, amelanistic and hypomelanistic.

Ecdysis: The process of shedding skin.

Ectotherm: An animal that cannot regulate its own body temperature.

Egg bound: A condition that prevents a female snake from laying her clutch of eggs. Typically it is from an infertile egg stuck to the lining of the oviduct.

Filial: Pertaining to the sequence of generations following the parental generation, each generation being designated by an F followed by a subscript number indicating its place in the sequence.

Force feed: To feed a snake by force.

Fuzzy: A young mouse usually 7-12 days old.

Genotype: The genetic make-up that produces a phenotype, and is passed down to offspring.

Gestation: The development of an embryo inside a female snake, meaning the ovum is already fertilized.

Gestation Period: The period between fertilization and egg laying or birth.

Gravid: Describing a female that is carrying eggs or young.

Hemipenis: The organ used by a male snake to deposit sperm inside a female's body during breeding season. Male snakes have two hemipenes(pl.) Males only use one at a time.

Herp: A term used within the hobby to describe reptiles and/or amphibians.

Herping: A term used to describe the process of looking for herp(s). [see herps]

Herper: A person who collects,breeds, or keeps herp(s). [see herps]

Heterozygous (het): Having to different alleles of a particular gene in a gene pair. For example, breeding between a hypomelanistic and a normal the offspring will all be normal with all the offspring carrying the hypomelanistic gene. These offspring will be called heterozygous or het hypomelanistic.

Homozygous: Having two identical alleles for a particular gene in a gene pair. For example, a hypomelanistic snake is homozygous for hypomelanism, as it carries two identical alleles.

Hopper: A juvenile mouse 12-19 days old.

Hybrid: The offspring between two snakes but not with in the same species.
Intergrade: A locale snake that is in the overlap area of two subspecies that may show characteristics of both subspecies.

Juvenile: A young snake, not yet sexually mature.

Glossary

Lacey Act: Federal Law enacted in 1900 and named after John Lacey. The Lacey Act protects both plants and wildlife by creating civil and criminal penalties for a wide array of violations, and most notably prohibits trade in wildlife, fish, and plants that have been illegally taken, transported or sold. The law is still in effect, although it has been amended several times.

Lateral: The side of the snake.

Locale: A specific area that an animal was captured.

Melanistic: Having excessive amounts of melanin or black coloration.

Mouth Rot: (Stomatitis) an infection in the lining of a snakes mouth, usually a bacterial infection and is treatable.

Musk: Foul smelling liquid produced by scent glands to deter predators away.

Neonate: Newly hatched snake.

Opaque: A term used to describe a snake when he has "cloudy eyes" right before the process of shedding it skin. This usually
takes place 7-10 days prior to shedding their skin.

Ophiophagous: Feeding on snakes.

Oviparous: Egg laying.

Ovum: Egg, prior to being fertilized.

Palpate: To feel for eggs with slight pressure on the ventral.

Phenotype: The visible characteristics of a snake.

Photoperiod: The length of daylight the snake is exposed to.

Pinkie: A newborn mouse 0-7 days old.

Pip: (pipping) The act of a snake poking its' head out of an egg.

Pop: This term is used to describe the process of sexing neonate snakes by inverting the male hemipenes.

Prey: A snake's food item.

Probe: An instrument used in the sexing of snakes, it is usually meds of surgical steal and has a ball on the end.

Recessive: Mutant genes that will change the wild phenotype snake to the mutant gene as long as two are present. If only one is
present the snake will be heterozygous and display its normal characteristics.

Regurgitate: To vomit.

Shed: See Ecdysis.

Subadult: A juvenile animal that is close to sexual maturity.

Subcaudal: The underside of the tail.

Taxonomy: Systematic naming of animals.

Thermal gradient: Gradual change in temperature.

Thermo-regulate: When a snake moves from one temperature zone to another.

Triad: Group of three rings.

Tricolor: A triad of 3 different colors, usually red, white/yellow and black.

Trio: Breeding group of 1 male and 2 females.

Vent: The opening at the end of the cloaca where bodily fluids are secreted.

Ventral: The belly of the snake.

Xanthic: Yellow color.

Weanling: A mouse that is 19-25 days old.

Vanished Pattern Tricolor

© Neil Little

Breeders & Other Resources

This section of the book is for the benefit of those that are looking to purchase captive-produced offspring and or related supplies. This is by no means a full listing, but can point any interested parties to breeders and other reptile related companies. This listing is a service to our readers and is not an endorsement to any particular person or company. Please use your own due diligence when purchasing captive-produced animals and/or reptile supplies and services.

Breeders

Scott Ballard (Illinois)

Scott Ballard has been keeping and breeding milksnakes since the late 1970s. He currently is working with Latin American milksnakes almost exclusively, and maintains most of those Mexican, Central and South American *triangulum* subspecies. Many of those that he works with are represented by more than one line, and Scott likes to keep those lines as pure as possible by not mixing any of the various subspecies. His email is snakesandpaws@earthlink.net

Shannon Brown (California)

Shannon has been breeding snakes ever since he was 16 years old. He has hatched just about everything from A to Z (*alterna to zonata*). He even named one of his six daughters "Zonata". He started with boas and pythons, but now specializes in mostly Honduran milksnake morphs and locality California and Gray-Banded kingsnakes. His original website, www.highsierrareptiles.com was first launched in 1996 and is undergoing a complete overhaul to be debuted soon. He can be reached at zonata@highsierrareptiles.com Phone- (760) 872-2847

Dell Despain (Montana)

Locality North American milk snakes are what Dell tries to stay focused on. Specifically Pale milk snakes (*Lampropeltis triangulum multistrata*), and Red milk snakes (*Lampropeltis triangulum syspila*).He also keeps a colony of Rubber boa (*Charina bottae*). Dell can be reached at kerstinbeijer@msn.com.

Terry Dunham (Kentucky)

Terry Dunham (of Albino Tricolors) no longer breeds snakes. But he produced Scarlet Kingsnakes, was an early pioneer of Honduran morphs, and produced numerous mutations of Mountain Kingsnakes. Parts of his website, albinotricolors.com, haven't been updated for several years, but the "genetics" part remains current and useful. His email is rtdunham@albinotricolors.com

Breeders

Mike Falcon (Florida)

Hondurensis aficionado for more than 30 years, and proprietor of Extreme hondurensis. Mike specializes in breeding specific genetically selected Honduran milksnake morphs, including the first Extreme Hypo (2001) and first Extreme Ghost (2005). His fascination for Honduran Milksnakes started back in the early 1990's when he was able to acquire some nice tangerine phase specimens from a wholesaler in Tampa..... and the rest is history. His contact info is: falconsnakefarms@msn.com

Rusty Green (Florida)

Rusty has been a nature lover as long as he can remember. His first pet snake, an Eastern Hognose, started a lifelong interest in reptiles. Rusty has bred various species of lizards, chameleons and snakes over the past 20+ years but has primarily focused on Honduran Milksnakes and Western Hognose in recent years. His e-mail is: rustingreen@hotmail.com

Cole Grover (Montana)

Specializing in locality-specific, wild-type Milk Snakes (*Lampropeltis triangulum*) and select morphs, Cole is located in south-central Montana. Working with a multitude of both temperate ("North of the Border") and Latin American forms, he strives to maintain the lineage and locality integrity of the animals. Cole has been keeping and breeding Milk Snakes since the mid-1990s and can be reached via e-mail at colegrover@gmail.com.

Neil Little (United Kingdom)

I first started keeping pythons back in 2004, but then changed direction and kept spiders and scorpions. However my passion for snakes never disappeared, and in 2008 I began keeping and breeding kingsnakes and milksnakes. My collection includes: California & Florida kingsnakes, Honduran Milksnakes and a few locality specific milksnakes . I can be contacted at littlekingsandmilks@hotmail.com, or visit his facebook page: littlekingsandmilks.

Breeders

Jonel Lopez (California)

Jonel Lopez has always been fascinated with animals in general from the very beginning coming from the Philippine Islands. In the last 20 years his primarily focus is in keeping and captive propagation of various types of snakes and with each passing year he finds himself learning more about his animals, new husbandry methods and techniques. He also is an avid field herper/photographer and enjoys learning the natural history of animals that he encounters in the wild. His email is tuklawjon795@hotmail.com.

Bill Love (Arizona & Florida)

Breeding hypo and 'tangerine dream' Honduran milk snakes is behind him, but Bill is still active in herping. He now concentrates on photography and writing, and leading eco-tours to see wild herps in Arizona and Madagascar. He markets his efforts on www.BillLovePhotography.com, www.ReptileRally.com and www.BlueChameleon.org . His email is bill@bluechameleon.org .

Douglas Mong - Serpentine Specialties (Florida)

I first started keeping varieties of snakes in 1966-67. Since those early years, I've worked with different boas, pythons, cornsnakes, ratsnakes, kingsnakes and different types of milksnakes. My main focus has always been working with colubrids. I currently work with Honduran milksnake morphs, central Guatemalan milksnakes, Yucatan milksnakes, Outer Banks kingsnakes, "high-yellow" Florida kingsnakes, and various corn and locality-specific ratsnake mutations. I can be reached at: dmong@coldbloodedpublishing.com
Visit my website at: serpentinespecialties.webs.com

Dave Niles (North Carolina)

Dave Niles has been interested in snakes his entire life and has kept snakes since he was 10 years old. Dave mainly keeps and breeds milk snakes, specializing in locality North American milksnakes. As well as locality Sinaloan Milksnakes and a few other select South American milks. Dave also has a very small colony of kingsnakes, boa constrictors and other colubrids. Dave can be reached at dnsreptiles@yahoo.com and his website address is www.freewebs.com/dnsreptiles.

Breeders

Steve Osborne; Professional Breeders (Montana)

With over 40 years of herpetoculture experience, Steve originated a number of Lampropeltis varieties that are popular in the hobby and business today, including the "Super Hypo" Honduran Milk Snakes. He currently focuses on the commercial breeding of Utah Banded and Arizona Reticulated Gila Monsters, several Kingsnake species, and Ball Pythons color and pattern morphs. Steve does not work with the Honduran Milk Snakes at this time. His website address is: www.probreeders.com and e-mail contact is probreeders@yahoo.com.

Reptile Basics (North Carolina)

Reptile Basics, Inc was established in 1994 by Rich Goldzung. They sell all your reptile equipment, caging, and supply needs. They carry a wide range of products that have stood the test of time and their customer service is second to none. Whether your a small hobbyist or large breeder Reptile Basics can handle it. They also wholesale supplies to other entities and manufacture some of their own products. You can reach them at www.reptilebasics.com.

Robert Seib (California)

I have worked with many different colubrids over the years, including Patternless Sinaloan Milksnakes, Hybino Honduran Milksnakes, Mandarin Ratsnakes and Eastern Indigos. Even though those species are behind me I am still currently working with various morphs of Ball Pythons and a couple other species. I can be reached by email @ rseib73@gmail.com.

Wayne Sanders (Nevada)

Selective breeder of colubrids for many years, building a solid reputation for pioneering and or establishing pinstriped Mexican milks, Cosala sinaloan milks, striped variations of the Honduran Milksnake and hypomelanistic Tarahumara Mountain Kingsnakes. With more exciting projects planned in the future. I can be reached at snakecellar@gmail.com

Breeders

Don and Sally Shores; Shores Enuff Snakes (Texas)

Producing captive-bred morphs of kingsnakes, milksnakes, cornsnakes, ratsnakes, Nelson's milksnakes, rosy boas, gopher and bullsnakes, and Glossy Snakes. They specialize in Honduran milksnake and Desert kingsnake morphs. Don and Sally have been breeding snakes for over 25 years, and are very selective with the animals they breed. They believe in quality and honesty. Visit their site at: www.shoresenuffsnakes.com Phone: (817) 246-5710

Jorge Sierra; Sierra Snakes (Florida)

Breeder of select colubrids since the early 90s. Involved with reptiles since the mid 70s. He keeps and breeds many different types of colubrids, but has been specializing in Florida Kings for the last 5 years. He also works with some unique combinations of Cornsnake morphs. His website is Sierrasnakes.com and can be contacted through the website, or by email at a153fish@aol.com

Tim Spuckler; Third Eye Herptile Propagation (Ohio)

Tim has been breeding snakes and selling them to the public for over two decades. He field herps extensively and has had several articles printed in "Reptiles" magazine. He works with a wide variety of reptiles and amphibians and under the name Third Eye Herptile Propagation produces milk, king, pine, garter and rat snakes. Visit his website at:
http://www.thirdeyeherp.com/

Thomas Steffen (Duisburg, Germany)

Starting in mid 80s with different colubrids, breeding different snakes since the early 90s including Indo-Australian pythons - since 2003 focus on Honduran Milksnakes, which are now present in collections in US and Europe.

For more information visit reptilienzucht.com or by email at thomas@reptilienzucht.com.

Breeders

Sunshine Serpents - owned by Daniel Parker (Florida)

Sunshine Serpents is a multifaceted company dealing with all things reptilian. In addition to breeding numerous species of snakes, turtles, and tortoises, Sunshine Serpents guides some of the only herp focused eco-tours in the United States, as well as educational presentations. Sunshine Serpents also offers wildlife photography and consultation for film and TV projects.

www.sunshineserpents.com

Stu Tennyson (Texas)

Like many, his interest in herpetology started at a young age. Through the years he has refined his interest down to a few species; milk snakes, gray banded kingsnakes and hognose snakes. He likes to spend as much time in West Texas not only looking for the snakes he loves but all the other critters and sights to see there. There's just something about the ambiance of the Chihuahua desert that attracts him.

See his collection at: www.facebook.com/stusherps
email: stuart.tennyson@gmail.com

Molli Thibodeaux (Louisiana)

Molli is a breeder of Western Hognose Snakes as well as a pre-vet/ biology major and a part-time artist. She has worked with animals all of her life, including exotics. For anyone interested in her artwork or snakes, she can be reached through email at mollithibodeaux@hotmail.com or by facebook at https://www.facebook.com/molli.thibodeaux

Tremendous Tricolors - owned by James Tintle (Florida)

Tremendous Tricolors produces quality captive bred snakes, and has a large assortment of various morphs and locale specific animals. They specialize in tricolor snakes. The diversity of their collection ranges from North American Milksnakes to South American Milksnakes but they also work with Tarahumara Mountain Kingsnakes, Durango Mountain Kingsnakes as well as select other snakes from the genus *Lampropeltis*.

email: jtintle@tremendoustricolors.com
phone: (813) 610-0729

Breeders

Nathan Wells (Texas)

Specializing in locality specific gray-banded kingsnakes, Mexicana Complex kingsnakes, Mexican and Latin American milksnakes, Brazilian rainbow & red tail boa constrictors and jungle carpet pythons. Rare Localities and Select Wild Types of all snakes.

email: natewells76@hotmail.com

Randy Whittington (North Carolina)

I've liked reptiles and amphibians for as long as I can remember. I began catching snakes and other herps in the woods and creek behind our home sometime in 1973 when I was eight years old. My parents were afraid I'd eventually pick up and be bitten by a venomous snake, so they bought me a red-tail boa the next year. They hoped it would stop me from catching and bringing home snakes, but it didn't work. I already had my first field guide and was hooked. My interest (especially in snakes) has only continued to grow ever since, eventually leading to keeping and breeding various species over the years. I produce different milksnakes, ratsnakes, kingsnakes, Pituophis ,boas and specialize in Asian ratsnakes. I can be contacted at: colubridman@nc.rr.com

Phone: (919) 418-4984

Index

A

abbreviations 127
aberrant 107–123
albino *See also* amelanistic
albumin 45–53
allele 56–63
Alloway, Jeff 86
amel *See also* amelanistic
amelanistic 64–89
Amikacin 146
anatomy 133–135
anery *See also* anerythristic
anerythristic 73
apical pits 132
arboreal 17
aspen 16–27
aspiration 143
Atlantic Central American Milksnake.
    See L.t.polyzona
axanthism 73

B

Bailey Line Aberrant 108
Bailey, Marc 108
balantidium 147
Baraducci, Joe 75
Barczyk, Brian 67
Baytril 146
Belize 137
Bell, Mark 76
bicephalic 122
binomial nomenclature 128
biting 35
Blair, Ric 121
Blanchard's Milksnake. *See L.t.blanchardi*
Blister Disease 152
braining 21
breeder 28–35
breeding behavior 40–53
Brown, Shannon 76
brumation 38–53
Burgundy 121

C

caging *See also* housing
calcification 45
Calico 121
calorie intake 26
Campeche 137
candling eggs 46–53
cannibalism 27
carbon dioxide 45
carotenoid 73–89
cedar shavings 16
ceramic heat emitters 17–27
cestodes 146
Chiapas 136
chromatophores 63
chromosome 56–63
ciliates 147
Ciprofloxacin 146
Clark, Guy 109
class 128–135
classification 128–135
cloaca 31
cloacal gaping 41
clutch 45–53
coconut bark 16–27
coconut peat 46
cold-blooded 38
copulation 41
Costa Rica 136
courtship 40–53
crystalline structure 74

D

Damm, Norm 108
data 126
deformities 122
diseases 142–153
Doherty, David 76
dominant gene 56
Dunham, Terry 56
dysecdysis 151
dystocia 42

E

ecdysis 12
ectoparasites 148
egg-bound. *See* dystocia
egg deposition 44
egg-laying 42
egg retention 143. *See* dystocia
El Salvador 136
embryo 45–53
enclosures 11–27
endoparasites 146

entamoeba invadens 147
erythrin 62, 73
erythrophores 63
European Line 111
expanded PVC 15–27
Exposito, Joe 96
external parasites. *See* ectoparasites
extreme ghosts 96
extreme hypo 84

F

Falcon, Mike 84
fecal matter 38, 147
feeding 19
Fenbendazole 147
fertilizers 47
flagellates 147
flagyl 148
Flexwatt 15
follicles 40
frozen thawed feeding 19

G

garden mulch 17
genetic possibilities 55–63
genetics 55–63
Gentamicin 146
genus 128–135
ghost 90–101
gravid 41
Green, Rusty 87
ground-dwelling *See also* terrestrial
growth rate 12–27
Guatemala 136
Guatemalan Milksnake *See L.t.abnorma*
Guy Clark Crazy Line 109

H

handling 33–35
Hatch Rite® 46
health issues 15
heat cable 15–27
Heating 17
heat mats 17–27
heat tape 15–27
hemipenes 41
hemipenis 41
herpetoculturists 47
het. *See* heterozygous
heterozygous 56–63
hide box 12–27
homozygous 56–63

Honduran Milksnakes
 captivity 10
 housing 11
Honduras 136
Hortenbach, Holger and Gabriele 67
housing 11
 housing hatchling 11
 housing subadults and adults 15
humidity 12–27
hybino 97–101
hypo *See also* hypomelanistic
hypoerythristics 74
hypomelanistic 80–89
hypoxanthic 73

I

illness 142–153
incandescent light bulbs 17–27
incubating medium 45
incubating temperatures 48
Incubation 42–53
infertile egg 44–53
inherited 55–63
internal parasite *See* respiratory infections
internasals 131
iridophores 74

J

Jacobson's organ 133
juvenile 33

K

Keasler, Gary 93
kingdom 128–135
Kooij, Jaap 111

L

La Libertad 137
Lambert, John 87
Lampropeltis 129
Lampropeltis triangulum hondurensis 129
Lampropeltis triangulum triangulum 129
Lampros 129
leathery shell 45
L.getula 27
L.g.splendida 119
Linnaeus, Carolus 128
live feeding 19
Love, Bill and Kathy 81
lowlands 38
L.t.abnorma 136
L.t.blanchardi 137

L.t.campbelli 119
L.t.oligozona 136
L.t.polyzona 137
L.t.stuarti 136

M

Maheuron, Terry 87
Mega Hypo 86
melanin 62
melanophores 63
meristics 130
meristos 130
metabolic processe 38
metabolism 39
metronidazole 148
mice 21
Michaels, Steve 121
mites 30, 148
Mong, Douglas 84
Montoya, Bob 93
morph 55
mouth rot *See* ulcerative stomatitis
musking 35
mutations 55–63

N

necrotic dermatitis 152
nematodes 146
neonate 53
nesting box 42
nesting medium 43–53
newborn mice. *See* also pinkies
newspaper *See* also substrate
Nicaragua 136

O

Oaxaca 136
opaque 15
Opferman, Regis 121
order 128–135
Osborne, Steve 81
ova 40
oviduct 143
ovum 56

P

Pacific Central American Milksnake.
    See L.t.oligozona
palpation 143
Panacur 147
parietals 131–135
Parker, Daniel 123

patternless 117
pattern, reverse 118
pearls 103–105
peat moss 46
peltis 129
perlite 47–53
pet shop 28
phenotype 73
pheromones 39
phylum 128–135
pigment cell *See* chromatophores
pigments 62
pin-banded 115
pine shavings 17
pinkies 23
pinworm 146
pipping 50
polygenic inheritance 106–123
popping 53
Porras, Louis 67
post-brumation 39
prefixes 63
    A 63
    An 63
    hyper 63
    hypo 63
pre-lay shed 43–53
probing 53
pteridines 63
Pueblan Milksnake 119
punnett square 60
purchase 30–35
purines 74

Q

quarantine period 31
Quintana Roo, Yucatan 137

R

rack systems 11–27
range map 136–141
rats 21
RBR *See also* red body rings
recessive gene mutations 56
record keeping 124
red body rings 91
regurgitate 35
Reptile shows 29–35
reptile suppliers 17–27
respiratory infections 145
rheostats 17–27
rhizopoda 147

R.I. *See* respiratory infections
Rice, Peter 111
rodent 26

S

Sanders, Wayne 108
San Luis Potosi 137
Scale Rot 152
scale tipping 65–89
scenting 23
seasonal changes 39
Seib, Robert 98
sexing hatchlings 53
shedding 12–27
shiny scale *See Lampros*
shiny shield *See Lampros*
shipment 31
Shores, Don 86
Shulse, Chris 118
snake hook 35
snow 99–101
sockhead 119
soldering gun 11
sperm 45
sperm ducts 41
sphagnum moss 12–27
spring (season) 39
Steffen, Thomas 111
string of pearls 40
Striped Aberrant 120
Stuart's Milksnake *See L.t.stuarti*
substrate 16
Super Hypo 81

T

Tabasco 137
Tangerine Dreams 81
taxonomy 128–135
tease-feeding 25
temperate gradient 18
temperatures 17
temporal band 131
Tennyson, Stu 78
terrestrial 17
thermal sensory organs 132
thermostat 15–27
trematodes 146
triangulum 129
trichomonas 147
triple homozygous *See* also pearls
Two-Headed *See* bicephalic

U

ulcerative stomatitis 144
ultra-light hypo 84
umbilical cord 53
uric acid 74

V

vanishing pattern 117
vent. *See* also cloaca
ventilation 47
Veracruz, Mexico 137
vermiculite 43–53
vesicular dermatitis 152
veterinary 143–153
viable egg 45
vivarium 15
V/P *See* also vanishing pattern

W

water bowl 18
water requirement 18
websites 30
Williams, Kenneth L. 130
worms 146

X

xanthic 73
xanthin 62
xanthophores 63

Y

yolk sac 53
Yucatan 137

www.ingramcontent.com/pod-product-compliance
Lightning Source LLC
Chambersburg PA
CBHW060809010526
44116CB00002B/22